FLORIDA STATE
UNIVERSITY LIBRARIES

MAY 2 4 2001

TALLAHASSEE, FLORIDA

Guerrilla TV

FLORIDA STATE
UNIVERSITY LIBRARIES

MAY 0 1 2001

TALLAHASSEE, FLORIDA

With particular thanks for help and encouragement to (in alphabetical order):

John Allen, David Bowen Jones, Rebecca Promitzer, and Melloney Roffe.

Guerrilla TV

Low Budget Programme Making

Ian Lewis

Focal Press

OXFORD AUCKLAND BOSTON JOHANNESBURG MELBOURNE NEW DELHI

PN
1992.75
.L44
2000

Focal Press
An imprint of Butterworth-Heinemann
Linacre House, Jordan Hill, Oxford OX2 8DP
225 Wildwood Avenue, Woburn, MA 01801-2041
A division of Reed Educational and Professional Publishing Ltd

℞ A member of the Reed Elsevier plc group

First published 2000

© Reed Educational and Professional Publishing Ltd 2000

All rights reserved. No part of this publication may be reproduced in
any material form (including photocopying or storing in any medium by
electronic means and whether or not transiently or incidentally to some
other use of this publication) without the written permission of the
copyright holder except in accordance with the provisions of the Copyright,
Designs and Patents Act 1988 or under the terms of a licence issued by the
Copyright Licensing Agency Ltd, 90 Tottenham Court Road, London,
W1P OLP, England. Applications for the copyright holder's written
permission to reproduce any part of this publication should be addressed
to the publishers

British Library Cataloguing in Publication Data
Lewis, Ian, 1962–
    Guerrilla TV: low budget programme making
    1. Television – Production and direction
    I. Title
    791.4'5'0232

Library of Congress Cataloguing in Publication Data
A catalogue record for this book is available from the Library of
Congress

ISBN 0 240 51601 X

This book has no connection with *The Guerrilla Film-makers'
Handbook.*

Composition by Genesis Typesetting, Rochester, Kent
Printed and bound in Great Britain by
Biddles Ltd, www.biddles.co.uk

FOR EVERY TITLE THAT WE PUBLISH, BUTTERWORTH-HEINEMANN
WILL PAY FOR BTCV TO PLANT AND CARE FOR A TREE.

Contents

Dear Diary,

Today the telephone rang. A voice announced 'Good News!' We had the money to make a series of six half-hour travel programmes in Europe. Starting as soon as we can. I asked how much money. '£25,000' says my colleague. To make six half-hours in Europe.

Oh, brave new world, that has such creatures in it.

But it can be done. We did it. We've done it before. And we've done it well. And this book will show you some ways to achieve high quality television for budgets that ought to send you screaming from the room. There are other ways; but I know that these methods have worked and do work for us.

Introduction

This book is about empowerment; about making things happen. I hope the New Producer will find a good deal of helpful material. But the Older Producer New to Tiny Budgets should also be able to benefit from perhaps a slightly different way of looking at the production process.

Anyone who needs or wants to make high quality television programmes – or films – on low budgets will find some ideas, inspiration, or help here. It's about achieving a big-budget look on a small budget production. It's a personal look at ways of doing it. There are hardly ever any single right answers. Your way is probably different from mine; but these are a few ideas to react to.

Perhaps you have been working for years in the 'traditional' environment of fully-staffed (or long-term contract) television stations, and now find yourself free to pursue a career whose boundaries are less well marked out than you're used to. One thing that will certainly be missing is the support services. There are no secretaries down the corridor, no edit suites or machine rooms where you can get a quick transfer done (even if the paperwork is horrendous); no libraries for research, and no archive an in-house telephone call away. This book assumes that its readers are starting with little more than a desk and a telephone, in a world where everything has to be paid for. Discovering the true cost of things can also come as something of a shock. The costing systems of many large companies bear little relation to the realities of production in the free world.

Or you might be quite new to the business of production. It's easy to turn a basically profitable situation into a financial loss through ignorance, or bad advice, carelessness, or simply bad luck. I hope this will help put some structure on the business, and show what is possible with a little thought.

And that will be a mantra through the whole book: *think before you spend*. Do not use money (of which you have very little) as a substitute for thought (which is free). And the other mantra: in the end, *you don't save money by scrimping*.

As technology has become cheaper (and also as budgets have dropped) a generation of videographers has grown: one-person bands who interview, shoot, write, and edit; basically producing a film or programme as author, all on their own. Some people are very good at it. I hope that people who work like this may find something in here, too, but this is not the book to tell you how to become a videographer. There are others which do that. The methods we use employ 'proper' traditional forces, in an extremely efficient way to maintain the kind of technical and editorial standards we've always been used to. This is not so much about video diaries, it's about (sometimes) glossy conventional programming of all sorts. My feeling is that if you can't do something really well yourself, then get someone else to do it for you.

The skills of film and television production involve thousands of tiny details, none of them particularly complex or difficult on their own. There are no magic wands. There's no simple single spell for making a $20 million action movie for $25. What follows is an approach which works for us. Not all of it may work for you – but at least you will have thought about it, and that's the most important starting point.

This is not a manual of basic production techniques (consult the publisher's catalogue for excellent examples of those) but a way of focusing techniques to produce high quality programming on low budgets.

PERSPECTIVES

The start of television in the UK: the BBC

During the working lifetime of some people still working in television, the UK has moved from having one television channel, to hundreds. The life of everyone in the country has been affected.

It's generally agreed that it was the BBC that launched the world's first regular commercial television service, in 1936. Television was a fabulous invention; but nobody quite knew what to do with it – certainly not the people in power at the BBC. Then the war intervened and the service stopped altogether.

In 1946, television started up again and, during the next ten years, gradually began to find its feet as a medium that was distinct from radio – more than simply a way of adding pictures to the programmes that audiences were already familiar and comfortable with.

The ethos of the BBC was then, and in many ways still is, dominated by the character of its first Director General, Lord Reith. The privilege of broadcasting carried tremendous responsibilities. The idea that any channel, whether radio or television, should exist entirely for entertainment was anathema. The BBC had a sacred duty to inform, educate, and – yes, entertain while doing so. In this world of public service broadcasting, the public were served by being given what they would want if only they were educated enough to ask for it, rather than what they said they wanted when asked. In those days they were never asked, in any case. It was the absolute antithesis of the focus-group, market-research led scheduling that came to dominate the end of the century.

Reith's idea of broadcasting and the duties of broadcasting were bred in him by the strict Scottish, puritan background he came from. You did things because they were the right thing to do. But the strength of his personality and his beliefs led to the development of an extraordinary organization, which produced programming unrivalled anywhere in the world for the consistency of its output – and, yes, it was popular.

Some would say that Reith's BBC was popular because it was a monopoly. It was the medium that people were attracted to, not so much the messages that were put out on it. Television after the war, too, was still very much the poor younger sibling of the far better established, far better funded radio networks.

Then, in 1954, an Act of Parliament was passed which would allow a second television channel – an independent television channel – and this was the real beginning of the world we're in today.

ITV was not to be a single television station, but a collection of regional stations, which would give viewers something completely different from the very London-centred, upper-middle class driven British Broadcasting Corporation. The Independent Television company in each region would receive a licence to broadcast for 12 years, after which the company's performance would be reviewed, and the licence renewed or not, as seemed appropriate to the newly-formed Independent Television Authority (ITA). The transmitters themselves were owned by the ITA, and each company would pay a rent for their use which depended on the size of the company and its available audience. The London companies paid millions, while Grampian paid only a few thousand pounds a year.

Just as important as the regional nature of the new channel was the way in which it was to be financed. The BBC was, and still is, financed by a licence fee levied on every household with equipment to receive its signals. In those days there were separate radio and television licences. Later the radio licence was dropped altogether. It's this licence fee which gives the BBC much of its power – and which is also its Achilles' heel. The BBC insists that it is not a government establishment (which, constitutionally, it isn't). It began as the British Broadcasting Company, not as a government department and fiercely contests any suggestion that it is influenced in any way by the current government – proving its point by routinely upsetting politicians, whoever they are.

None the less, the BBC owes its existence to a Royal Charter, and the level of the licence fee to a government decision. In truth the BBC is only as independent as the establishment (in the wider sense) allows it to be. Periodically, the charter comes up for renewal. At these times, there is no theoretical reason why the BBC should not be disbanded, broken up, or reconstructed. The level at which the licence fee is set, too, obviously determines what the BBC is able to do – because until relatively recently *there was no other money*. It could be argued that one of the reasons behind the passion with which the BBC has entered the digital, international marketplace is to assure more of its independence from government.

To return to ITV. The BBC is funded by a compulsory subscription. Households would not pay up another subscription for ITV, so there had to be some other way to finance the new television channel. And it was obvious – particularly if you took a glance across the Atlantic – that the way to do it was to permit advertising. Not too much. Only something like 6 minutes an hour. And let's keep the advertisers and the programme-makers well apart. We don't want anything happening like the soap operas (sponsored by soap-powder manufacturers) that we see in the United States.

This might seem like an odd way of describing advertiser-funded television, but it was more or less the way the thinking went. This is important, because it underlies many of the structures and attitudes that we still have in our television system.

ITV

ITV was founded to provide another source of entertainment and education. Unlike the BBC, the new television companies were permitted to finance themselves in any way they could; but in practice, the only real way open to them was through the selling of airtime to advertisers. The amount of advertising airtime permitted was very low. And the advertisers were not allowed to sponsor or produce programmes. Even now, the rules on sponsorship are very strict, although they're gradually being relaxed. The BBC's culture of editorial independence – of 'nobody tells us what to put in our programmes' – carried through into the new commercial world of ITV; and it's still there. And it's in the newer channels, too, if you look. It permeates the entire broadcasting establishment of Britain, because most people running or working in even the newer channels have grown up in a world where that is the case.

The most important and exciting times in television's history have been dominated by a very small number of individuals who have shaped a whole era. Television is, of course, full of talented and imaginative people, but probably less than a dozen names really shaped the history of the medium in this country. Reith is the first. The birth of ITV in May 1955 brought two more into the group: Sydney Bernstein, who ran Granada Television; and Lew Grade, of ATV, both of which were among the first ITV stations to begin broadcasting.

These men were very similar, and quite different. Sydney Bernstein came from a serious theatre-owning and producing family. Lew Grade's background was music hall and variety.

Between them, they turned television into a serious medium with its own rules and its own conventions.

If the BBC took much of its programming from the theatre, the new ITV was led right from the start by showbiz. If the BBC could trace its sensibilities back to Shakespeare; ITV was descended from music hall. Indeed, many variety acts which would have disappeared completely found new life in television. Only in the late 1980s did the music hall traditions of the nineteenth century finally die out. Think of Morecambe and Wise, Tommy Cooper, Little and Large.

But it wasn't just in light entertainment that ITV took a fundamentally different approach from their pre-cursors at the BBC. ATVs 'Armchair Theatre' series of made for TV – and more important *written* for TV – was arguably the beginning of television drama as an art form in its own right. Produced by a Canadian, Sidney Newman, it took its paradigms from the movies, not from the drawing room stage plays so beloved of the BBC.

The result of this totally different approach (combined with the novelty of having a choice at all) was that the BBC lost 70 per cent of its audience in the months following the launch of ITV.

ITV was structured as a collection of regional television stations. In practice, of course, the smaller stations had neither the financial nor the physical resources to provide a full-time channel of their own. So the ITV networked most of their programmes, with regional programming 'opt-outs'. Again, although theoretically each of the 14 stations could have delivered an equal share of ITV's network programming, in practice only the largest were able to contribute a significant amount. Income was derived entirely from advertising; and advertising revenue was limited by the 'cost per thou' – the rates charged per thousand viewers for the programme. Channel Television, with only 25,000 homes, couldn't possibly compete with the London stations.

So, although the Network Committee was theoretically composed of the managing directors of all 15 stations, in reality all the decisions were made by the companies who provided most of the programming. By the end of the 1960s this had become formalized into the 'big five' (by then): Granada, ATV, Thames, London Weekend, and Yorkshire. They decided what went on the network, and they provided practically all the programmes. The middle range companies – Anglia, Scottish, TVS, HTV, Ulster – could kick up a fuss and make sure they achieved some access to the network occasionally. But the small companies – Westward, Channel, Grampian, Border, Tyne-Tees – had no chance except on very rare occasions.

TV news

It's worth taking a small step to the side to consider television news as a separate issue, because what has happened to the way international news is delivered shows what is happening to other programming.

News is a special case because it's expensive, and because it's time-critical. A picture worth a front page and £1 million this morning is worthless tomorrow.

Everyone's horizons expanded after World War II. Many people had become used to travel. And parts of the world had become familiar from news of the war that had previously been only exotic, faraway dreams. And the power of moving pictures actually being delivered into your home, was unbeatable. So it was natural that television news – picture-led – should become important. And because it was picture-led, systems had to be set up to film events as they happened and (often the hardest part of the job) get the film back to broadcast it as quickly as possible. It's a much harder job and a much more expensive job than even press and radio had.

The problem that all news organizations always have is getting to the story while it's still going on.

So, as television news became more important, two things happened in 1955. The ITV companies formed a company jointly owned by all 15 of them to provide a news service to the ITV network: Independent Television News, and joined with United Press International to form an international news agency, known as UPITN.

The BBC joined with Reuters, NBC in New York, ABC in Australia, and BCNZ, the New Zealand national broadcaster, to form the British and Commonwealth Newsfilm Agency. This shortly changed its name to Visnews. Much later, Reuters bought out all the other partners, and the company is now called Reuters Television.

These two London-based agencies, Visnews and UPITN, dominated television news around the world for the next 40 years. Their only competition was a smaller agency run by the American broadcaster CBS.

They did this because they were all there was, not through any overt – or even conscious policy of cultural imperialism. Hardly any broadcasters, anywhere, can afford to provide themselves with their own worldwide news operation. What they do is subscribe to an agency for most of their foreign news and send their own crews if they can afford it and if the story gets big enough. This means that the world-view of television in Amman or Djibouti or Jakarta, was hugely influenced by the opinions of the London-based journalistic establishment and their views of what was important or interesting in the world events. It doesn't have to be a conscious desire to force a world-view on others. Any group of people inevitably develops a consensus view. It's just that a London-based view is bound to be different from a Harare-based view. A view which seems sincerely objective to you may not seem so to your friend across the river – and vice versa. When John Kennedy Jr died in his light aircraft, the news dominated not only the news media of the United States, but those of Britain, and much of Europe. The amount of coverage given to the story was, frankly, astonishing. Was it really a story of such crucial interest to the people of Europe? Many of them had never even heard of this particular Kennedy until his life ended. Or was this a particularly good example of how something which is – objectively – the lead story amongst the newsmakers of one country can leave the rest of the world mystified?

Television news was a global business (in terms of audiences) not because the whole world wanted news stories selected and provided by a western view of the world, but because that was all that was available. No-one could afford anything else. Several attempts were made over the years, mainly by groups in the developing world, to set up rival organizations. Only recently with the spread of available technology has this begun to happen.

This is important to us all, because it's a reminder that a global market is composed of hundreds of local markets; and this is a discussion we'll return to.

Meanwhile, back in 1960s Britain . . .

Quite simply, television found its feet in Britain during the 1960s. TV became a vigorous, different, exciting place to work. A new medium doing things that could only be done in television. The atmosphere was akin to the Hollywood of the late teens and early twenties; to the playhouses of London at the close of the sixteenth century. And this atmosphere was influenced by the Director-General of the BBC at the time, Hugh Carlton Greene (not to be confused with the antipodean game-show host). Having learnt their lesson from the sound beating the new ITV had given them, the BBC under Greene became a place which invented a particular kind of popular public service television. He was brilliant because he created an atmosphere which encouraged experiment; which dared to try things out. Not everything succeeded. It never can. But, together, the things which did succeed changed television for ever. If there was ever a golden age, it was then.

Programmes like *The Wednesday Play* invented a whole new genre of socially committed drama. *Cathy Come Home* had real social impact – a TV play actually changed the way homeless people were treated in the real world. Peter Watkins made two of the most powerful drama-docs ever, *The War Game*, so realistic it was banned from broadcast for twenty years; and *Culloden*. *Monitor* made serious arts accessible to everyone. *Talking to a Stranger* told the same story over four weeks, each week from the viewpoint of a different protagonist. That could only happen on television – not so much the techniques on the screen, but the use of scheduling, and the fact that programmes were brought to you in your home. Television is the art of organization. And *Z Cars*, a half-hour police drama series, probably the most revolutionary of all these ideas. It had never been done before, and it revolutionized both scheduling and production techniques.

Many of the most successful people in television and in cinema began their careers in the television industry of those days: Mike Newell and Michael Apted at Granada; Ken Russell at the BBC; Ken Loach and Tony Garnett who made *Cathy Come Home*.

This is important because it's a complete contrast to the situation we have now. Not because of the overall quality of the programmes. I'm sure we'd laugh at the naivety and clumsiness of many of these shows if we saw them now, and we make good programmes now, too. But you can only invent things once. You can be the first only once. We carry the legacy of these people willy nilly in what we consider to be the basic grammar of what we do – even if we see our purpose in life as being the destruction of that basic grammar.

More important than that, though, is the fundamental change that has led to the need for this book at all. In those days there were two channels, and everyone who watched television watched the same kind of television, and usually the same shows. It's not a statement about a lost 'community' except to say that then, for a short while, it was possible to change the world through television. Now there are so many channels and so many programmes that nothing can have that kind of influence ever again. And so the very real feeling of corollary responsibility is in danger of disappearing too.

In fact, this golden age of 'community' when everyone watched the same programmes was relatively short-lived. It wasn't until the late 1960s that you could say that most households possessed a television set. Television began as a very elitist medium, because television sets were very expensive. Interestingly, the price of a standard size television set has remained at around £300 for more than thirty years. £300 isn't such a lot now. It was a much more significant proportion of annual income in 1970, when a new graduate could expect to earn roughly £1200 a year.

BBC2

By the end of the 1960s not only had television grown up as a medium, the technology had begun to take enormous leaps forward. The launch of BBC2 in 1964 permitted the BBC two things, both of them of massive importance to the television industry.

Firstly, BBC2 was an important technical evolution of television. Until now, television in Britain had been broadcast in the so-called 'high-definition' format of 405 lines, in monochrome only, in the VHF radio band – the same as used for FM radio. Colour television had existed for some years in the United States, and was obviously what everyone wanted, but there are significant engineering problems in transmitting acceptable colour pictures in the VHF 405 line format. BBC2 was broadcast from the start only in 625 lines, and from 1967 in PAL colour – the first regular colour television service in Europe – broadcast in the UHF (ultra-high frequency) band. That remained the basic transmission format for television until the launch of digital terrestrial transmission – of which more later.

As with all channel launches which also involve new technology, practically nobody was able to watch it, but it was the beginning of the end for black and white television, and for 405 line transmissions.

The other effect of BBC2 was just as significant. In adding a second outlet, BBC2 provided the BBC with a place to put all the programming that its public service remit (and convictions) required it to make, but which didn't get the kind of audiences that competing programmes on ITV were getting. BBC2 was always intended to be a specialist channel. The kind of channel you chose to watch, rather than sitting back and enjoying the 'chewing gum for the eyes' of mainstream TV. In short, BBC1 became available to provide some real primetime competition to ITV. And the battle for audiences between BBC1 and ITV shaped the broadcasting of the next twenty years. The obligations to public service broadcasting became progressively eroded as the need to attract large audiences became greater and greater.

ITV needed to attract large audiences in order to earn the money to make programmes. Only with high ratings can advertisers be persuaded to pay out the extraordinary sums they did (and do) pay to get their message on air. But ITV was a ratings success from the start. The phrase 'a licence to print money' referred to the ITV of the late 1950s. The reason the BBC saw (and still sees) the need to compete on the same terms, is that they feel that only if they offer a truly mainstream service can they justify the licence fee – which is, after all, levied on everyone whatever television they watch.

It is also argued, of course, that precisely because the BBC has an income guaranteed by the licence fee, it has no need to chase audience share aggressively. It should rather retreat into providing the kind of high quality programmes that people didn't know they wanted to watch, rather than giving them what they say they want to see.

This is an argument which goes round endlessly. Take your pick on which side you prefer. What's important here is the effect that it has on all of us working in the industry. It won't be over until the BBC's licence fee is abolished, leaving this kind of programming to be produced only by voluntary-subscription television – as it is in the United States by PBS, the Public Broadcasting System. The problem is that PBS barely survives in the USA, with a population of 500 million. It's unlikely that a similar service could exist as any kind of a producing entity in our country with a tenth of the population. But then, finding ways around this kind of problem is what this book is about.

The 1980s

The end of the 1970s was also the end of the 'classic' world of British television, with a comfortable duopoly (the BBC and ITV) responding to each other in a more or less closed world. It was also the end of fully self-financed 'really big' event programming: works like *World at War, Brideshead Revisited, Holly-wood*, from ITV; *The Six Wives of Henry VIII, The Ascent of Man, Life on Earth*, from the BBC. A few of these were produced into the 1980s, but really the heart (and the money) had gone out of the business.

Licences

One of the reasons (a cynic might say it was *the* reason) for the flowering of ITV creativity and spend on high-budget, high-profile programming at the end of the 1970s was that the programme contractors' (the ITV companies') licences were due for renewal in 1982. The first round of licence renewals, in 1968, had seen changes in the network. There was no doubt that there would be further changes in 1982, if only to prove that the Independent Broadcasting Authority (the IBA, as the ITA was now called, to recognize the fact that since 1975, it was the controlling authority for commercial radio, too) really did have some teeth, and wasn't simply the lap-dog under the control of the big five ITV companies.

Changes were made: ATV (one of the big five) was deemed not to have served its regional audiences well enough; but in a curious compromise, the company only 'sort of' lost its licence. After some boardroom re-structuring, and the promise to open a studio centre in Nottingham, the company was renamed Central Television, and continued much as before. There were bigger changes amongst the other companies: The South of England lost Southern Television and the licence was awarded to Television South (TVS), who promised to open a studio centre in Maidstone to show that they cared more about the Eastern end of their region, and weren't leaving Kent and Sussex to the London broadcasters; and Westward Television lost to Television South-West (TSW).

So it all looked much like business as usual – a few changes in detail, but the same sort of people doing the same sort of work. But under the surface enormous changes were happening, though it was going to be a decade before they really showed.

Channel 4

The most obvious change in the broadcasting map of Britain was the opening of Channel 4 in 1982. Throughout the 1970s, a number of groups had been campaigning for a second independent channel – a kind of ITV equivalent to BBC2. The people campaigning for this channel had something more radical in mind than ITV2, however. They wanted it to be an *independent* channel, not just a commercial one. And, through it, they wanted to open up access to television to people outside the (by now) somewhat cosy duopoly of the BBC and ITV. To independent film-makers, for instance, who didn't feel that there needed to be such a rigid dividing line between people who worked in television, and people who worked in film.

In 1977 the Annan report – an independent government review of the broadcasting industry – supported the foundation of a fourth network, and finally, the channel went on air in 1982, with a completely new model of operation (for this country, at any rate).

The channel was always intended to be a 'minority' channel. It was not expected (or supposed) to collect a large audience share.

Obviously the only practical way of financing it was by advertising, but advertisers, who paid rates based on the 'cost per thou' were clearly not going to pay vast amounts of money to advertise to what was by definition a small audience. So, in another British compromise, a levy was made on the ITV companies, to finance Channel 4, and guarantee a minimum income for its operations.

Instead of constructing a massive studio centre, and employing thousands of people to produce all its own programmes, Channel 4 was (and is) a so-called 'publisher-broadcaster'. Channel 4 employees manage the funds, but the programmes are made under contract by other companies, and simply broadcast by Channel 4, in the same way that a book publisher decides on what books are to be published, but the books are not written by the publisher's staff.

There was some doubt as to whether there were actually enough independent producers in Britain to supply a whole new channel. A number of people expected ITV to provide most of the programming – and it did supply a large amount. But in fact a whole new branch of the industry sprang up, as if from nowhere. Channel 4 is obviously crucial to the rise of the independent production arm of the business in Britain; but its importance is as much as a catalyst, in providing a world in which independent production can exist, as in employing producers and production companies directly.

This book is about and for independent producers; we'll return to the 'Rise of the Indie' in a little while.

Meanwhile, around 1980, two other events occurred. Neither of them seemed terribly significant at the time to people working in television, but between them they ended the cosy duopoly – the Golden Age, some would say – and created the world we're in now.

In Britain, the Conservative Party won the general election, and Margaret Thatcher became Prime Minister.

The story of Thatcher's Britain is stale news. The world became weary of hearing the bleating of British television people: writers, producers, directors – about life in Thatcher's Britain. The day-to-day details are not important. What is important is the way in which the culture of the financial institutions of City of London altered completely during the decade. The endemic short-termism of the British banking system (something else that greatly concerns independent producers) became exaggerated beyond belief. Fortunes were made and lost several times in a single day. And new technologies played a massive part in this change. The crash of 1987 would not have been possible without new communications and trading technologies because the markets could not have reacted quickly enough to panic. In fact it was computers dealing on their own as programmed that caused much of the trouble.

This is relevant to us because this complete change in the idea of what a company – any company – is for affected television internally and externally. The old ITV made lots of money, true, but the culture was still that of public service. Perhaps it didn't seem so at the time, but the contrast with later is stark. That didn't mean dull and worthy programming, but it did mean programmes of high quality, whether light entertainment or arts.

By the end of the 1980s, the culture of ITV had turned round. No longer were the companies programme-makers and broadcasters funded by advertising. They were companies making money for their boards and shareholders, and they happened to make money by owning television stations. It wasn't an absolute change, that came later, but it was a big change.

And Thatcher's government, seeing that there were not only opportunities in ITV for making tremendous amounts of money, but also that now there was a much more active financial world which was interested in partaking of this feast, decided to sell the licences instead of giving them away. ITV stations were up for auction. Naturally the winners would have to be credible recipients (the so-called 'quality threshold'), but basically the government was cashing in.

This story continues, and we'll return to it; but basically the auctions for the licences of 1992 destroyed the old ITV, and changed the working environment of television forever: the environment of all television in Britain, including the BBC. The BBC is not and was not immune to change in ITV, because it compels itself to use BBC1 to compete directly with ITV. For all its faults, the ethos of a kind of commercial version of public service broadcasting still survived in the 'old' ITV. Now it was gone.

CNN

The other event of such significance? In 1980, far away in the deep south of the United States, Ted Turner launched a company called the Cable News Network.

Cable was much more widespread in the USA than in Europe, because it was the best way of delivering television to a largely urban population in a big country. CNN was a first, not only because it was the world's first 24-hour news channel, delivered to Cable television operators across the United States, but because it was delivered from Atlanta by satellite. It was slow to catch on. By the end of its first five years of life, CNN had lost more than $70 million. But Ted Turner believed in his vision; even though he described CNN as 'haemorrhaging red ink', he had the belief in his vision (and the financial resources) to keep going. CNN was an example of technological innovation, and of faith in an idea that influenced the whole world. The influence of its content – the continuous availability of news – on the wider world was also impossible to ignore.

CNN was important because it was (to all intents and purposes) the first dedicated cable television channel. Cable television existed in North America, and in various towns and cities throughout the world, including Britain, mainly as a way of distributing normal terrestrial television. The appearance of programming which was only available through cable changed the whole business. Where Ted Turner led, others followed: HBO, Nickelodeon, Arts & Entertainment, Showtime, MTV – are all cable (and later satellite) channels. These names are so familiar that we forget what a revolution in the industry of the early 1980s they represented. The total power of the major networks was broken for ever. No longer were they the only decision makers of the programmes that were made and shown. The digital revolution of the end of the twentieth century brought about a similar wave of democratization, and is at the heart of the need for this book.

In Britain, cable companies had begun producing local television programming during the late 1970s, in Milton Keynes, Swindon, and Westminster. It was a brave attempt, but there was never enough money, and the viewership was never large enough. The channels withered and died. Some broader form of distribution was needed – but the ideas were years ahead of the available technology.

Sky Television

In 1980, a producer at Thames Television called Brian Haynes made a programme about satellite television, and sold himself the idea. He managed to find backing for a company which he called *Sky Television*, and by 1982 was transmitting $1\frac{1}{2}$ hours a day to cable television in the UK and Scandinavia.

At this stage nobody knew whether Sky Television was an enthusiasts' folly, or whether it was the beginning of the future. As CNN was showing, a small company with limited resources was unlikely to last long enough to find out.

But Rupert Murdoch had seen Sky Television, and began to buy into it. By 1984, he owned it completely, and it was relaunched as the *Sky Channel* – still a satellite to cable service, but spreading as cable slowly spread through Britain.

There's no need to include every step in the process. Direct Broadcast by Satellite (DBS) to the home began at the end of the 1980s with a typically British muddle. Murdoch did not get the official licence, but continued transmissions anyway. Finally the 'official' company *British Satellite Broadcasting* folded, was taken over by Sky, and became BSkyB. The failure of BSB had much to do with its choice of the wrong technology. Instead of being compatible with a standard which was already established, even if only in a minor way, they decided to go for a different satellite transmitting in a different signal format, requiring all their subscribers (many of whom may already have been satellite enthusiasts) to buy new equipment to watch the programmes. Not enough people did.

The lesson seems to have been learnt at last. At the end of the 1990s, the spread of digital satellite and terrestrial television was ensured by giving away the equipment. Certainly, subscribers had to pay their subscriptions; but the equipment was free. There were effectively no start-up costs, always a major obstacle to change.

By the mid 1990s, Murdoch's BSkyB could be said to be a success. But Murdoch, like Ted Turner, had made massive losses year after year, because he believed in an idea, and believed in backing it for the long run. If these men had had the classic British requirement for a rapid and high rate of return on their investment, television would be quite different. Murdoch is not welcomed everywhere with equal warmth – but you have to admire and respect his vision and tenacity.

The new ITV

The licence renewals of 1992 brought about a massive change in the structure and culture of ITV. The auction was run by a secret bidding process. Since there was always the 'safety net' to decision making of the quality threshold, it's still hard to see the justification for this. It meant that companies had no idea what they were bidding against. Major franchises were won with bids of a few thousand pounds; fairly minor ones cost millions, which meant that the winning company was almost certainly not going to survive until the next bidding round. One of the biggest shocks was that Thames Television lost the London weekday licence – possibly so that the IBA could prove that it had the power to destroy one of the 'big five' companies.

An ITV Network Centre was created to control the scheduling and programming of the network and remove it from the power of the programme contractors, who now only had absolute power over the regional programmes they were still required to make.

The independent production sector was shaken up completely. On the one hand, three companies (Carlton and Meridian, which were new broadcasters; and HTV, which had decided to divest itself of most of it staff) had proclaimed they were to be publisher-broadcasters on the Channel 4 model. This certainly meant more opportunities for independent producers – or did it? As the programme controller of one of the biggest companies said to me at the time 'We're all independents, now.' With the ITV television companies competing for slots with the ITV Centre with everyone else, they hadn't much interest in working with independent producers.

On top of this, the employment market was suddenly awash with skilled people who had been made redundant from the ITV companies. In previous licence rounds, the incoming company (if there was a change) had more or less just taken over all but the most senior of the staff and the equipment of the outgoing company. In some parts of the country there were no other television technicians available, anyway. Now a combination of Thatcherite downsizing, and the new decision to be publishers rather than producers, meant that a fairly large number of people in a fairly small industry became 'unexpectedly available for the summer season', in the words of *The Stage*. So the expected bonanza didn't happen.

The 1990s

What did happen during the 1990s was exactly what the industry predicted, but the government and regulatory bodies had tried to prevent. Since the ITV companies now existed in the open market, it was logical to expect them to start buying each other up. Obviously, this would make nonsense of the idea of regional television, and the kind of federal network that ITV had always been, so the licence rules forbade any buying or selling for at least three years from the beginning of the licence period.

This had the effect of slowing up programme production, because all the companies were preparing fighting funds – and because, at the beginning of a licence period, they had nothing particular to prove. Just as at the end of the previous period, since the results were going to depend on cash, not on brownie points (from glossy, high-quality programming) there wasn't the same flood of exciting new programmes that there had been at the end of the 70s and early 80s. There was no point in trying to impress the ITC, because that wasn't what counted. What you needed to do was accumulate cash for the auction. So this whole auction process produced a gap in the production of programmes to impress for at least five years. Well, actually it produced a gap which meant that the old culture never returned.

And at the end of the embargo period, ITV boardrooms were like a chicken coop when the fox got in, as every company re-aligned itself, was bought up, or bought others.

The market ruled, as it was expected to. One of the justifications for the auction of licences and the setting up of the ITV Network Centre was to break the stranglehold on the network exercised by the big five. It worked. By the end of the 1990s, the stranglehold was exerted by the big three: Carlton, which by then owned Central, and Westcountry; Granada, which also owned London Weekend, and Yorkshire (which had already bought Tyne-Tees); and the United Media group, which didn't even have a licence in its own right, which owned Meridian, Anglia, and HTV. Only Scottish Television remained independent.

The relatively stable system of 'old ITV' died in 1992. This was combined with the changes in social attitudes to employment – led by the Thatcher government's determination to destroy the trade unions – and the ideas of the purpose of a company. During the 1980s and 1990s, the short-termism of British financial life extended to most companies of all sizes. Companies exist for the enrichment of their shareholders (and the board of directors). 'If we can exist without employees at all', they say, 'then we shall. Companies needed to be lean and mean.' Apart from anything else, the wider social costs of rising unemployment were not considered. This affected the BBC's outlook, too, and had the dramatic but unexpected side effect of gradually removing a knowledge base from television.

The culture of the film and television industry in Britain, in complete contrast to that of most of the rest of the world, is one of informal apprenticeship. That is, you learn how to do the job by working. In Europe (and, to a lesser extent, in the USA) you were expected to have gone to a film school of some sort and to have become 'qualified' through a course of education. Film schools and media courses are still not really seen by the film and TV industry in Britain as providing a useful practical qualification for work in the industry. What used to happen was that there was a kind of informal but none the less industry-standard career structure. You'd start as an assistant or some other lowly grade in a television company, and gradually work your way up, working on lots of programmes, gaining experience – and an unconscious 'feel' for the way things were done – as you worked.

Suddenly we had an industry where even the biggest companies were trying to get rid of all but the most essential staff, or work entirely through freelancers; where any formal in-house training courses were scrapped; where people were expected somehow to find out for themselves how to do things – but where the likelihood of them working anywhere that would give them the kind of concentrated and varied experience that the 'old' system would have given them was non-existent – because there wasn't anywhere.

And the problem was bound to get worse over time as people who had been made redundant left the industry, and as the skill base simply grew older. The problem isn't that only the old ways are the good ways. Of course people who have grown up in the 'new' world can make films and programmes as well as people from the 'old'. But it's much harder to start out. Not so hard to get *some* work; but much harder to get continual work, and so gain a solid perspective on the industry.

As usual, the BBC makes many noises about its independence, and its freedom to do what it wants and not be driven by the requirements of advertisers to deliver large audiences. And as usual, during the late 1980s and the 1990s, the BBC followed the trend. Under the leadership of John Birt, another of the half-dozen most influential people in British television, the BBC metamorphosed from a largely self-sufficient, programme-orientated organization which nurtured creativity in ways unparalleled in the world – into a mean, management-orientated, market-research led commercial organization, where those of the creative staff who remained (not having been sacrificed to the god of efficiency) lived in uncertainty, depression, and the grind of completing yet more paperwork before they could get down to the studio (or wherever).

Channel 5

In an attempt to counteract the way in which television was settling back into the effective duopoly of the old days, and to counter the attractions of satellite television (there was something of a political battle going on with Rupert Murdoch, whose influence tended to be seen by the establishment as somewhat malign) the government decided to award a franchise for a fifth terrestrial channel – through another bidding process.

By the time the winning company began broadcasting, at the end of March 1997, Channel 5 was already a bit of an irrelevance. The world had moved on. But it was another publisher-broadcaster to provide a theoretical outlet for independent production.

Why was it irrelevant? The thinking behind it was out of date. It was intended to broaden a picture of broadcasting which was inherited from the 1970s. The world wasn't like that any more. Satellite and cable television were already making a significant impact on viewing habits when the bidding process for Channel 5 began. By the time the channel launched, more people were watching satellite television than Channel 5. In fact, it's somewhat ironic that its terrestrial transmission reach was so limited (particularly in the south of England, where the available frequencies over-lapped with those of French broadcasters, so the Channel 5 transmitters could only transmit at very low power levels) that the only way it could reach a truly national audience was by being carried on BSkyB's satellite.

Digital television

1999 was the beginning of the end for nearly everything we've been talking about. In the early 1950s, you watched the BBC if you wanted to watch television, because that's all there was. Later you had two channels to choose between. By 1997 you (theoretically) had five choices, unless you were one of the minority to have invested in satellite television. Most viewers, however, remain conservative, and stuck with what they could receive free (apart from the licence fee, which was not optional) without making any changes to their receiving equipment.

Then digital television began broadcasting – both from satellite and from terrestrial transmitters.

Digital television is an example of technology leading events. Its appearance seems as inexorable as the spread of colour television in the 1970s, but it changes people's ideas of television so completely, that few people are sure how best to handle it. The only thing that can be said for certain is that the world of television (in the broadest possible sense) up to the turn of the century, and the world of television afterwards will bear only superficial resemblance to each other.

A major selling point of digital television is higher quality sound and pictures. This is a possible benefit – though it ain't necessarily so. The real difference is in the multiplicity of channels it can provide.

Satellite television began in the traditional programming mode, with general programming channels. Sky One is still such a channel. But as the number of channels available on satellite grew (as it had on cable before) the channels became increasingly specialized: a music channel; a rock music channel; a channel of special interest to women; a sports channel (actually it's always sports that lead new channel launches); a wildlife channel – and so on.

Digital broadcasting, whether from a satellite, or from terrestrial transmitters, increases the number of available channels several hundred fold. And all that available capacity is being used in ways that were unimaginable even ten years ago. Even the simplest use of this sudden over-capacity, the use of six or so channels to run the same film with staggered start times, so that you're never more than 15 minutes from the beginning of the film (what a waste of space!) is a small revolution.

Different camera angles from the same football match on different channels are often also offered. Far more creative uses of this capacity are being devised all the time.

OK. So we now have 250 channels to watch instead of four or five. What's the difference? Just that there's more of it?

The difference is massive, because it shifts the balance of power from the broadcaster to the viewer. When there were only one or two channels to watch, basically you took what the broadcasters decided you were going to have, or you went to weed the garden instead. With a choice of 250 channels you never have to weed the garden again. If you want to watch television, there will always be a programme somewhere that will interest you. You might have a problem finding it, but that's a different debate. Traditional general programming channels may disappear altogether. We don't know yet.

Whatever happens it's certain that the broadcasters are having to split their programming between various 'brands'. Audiences are not going to watch BBC1 any more, just because it's BBC1. The market (for audiences) is increasingly lead by content, and not by source. Viewers choose what they want to watch, and don't really care where it comes from.

That makes it very difficult for everyone. In order to keep their position in the market, broadcasters are fragmenting their output in to different channels. It's difficult for advertisers, who find themselves without the easy guarantee of everyone watching together, and who certainly aren't going to pay the kind of prices for maybe 100,000 viewers, that they paid for 10 million. It makes it very difficult for programme-makers. Because although the number of available channels has increased in ways unimaginable before, the total amount of money spent on producing programmes for television has hardly increased at all. At a time when the average cost of running ITV was around £250,000 per hour, there were satellite channels whose overall budget was £2500 per hour. Yes, a hundredth part. The challenge for producers like you and me is to find ways of making programmes for (and money from) those poorer channels.

Interactive television

We've become used to television as a one-way medium. They put it out. We watch it. 'Interactive television' in its widest sense, allows the audience to answer back – normally through a telephone data link going back to the broadcaster or cable station. This answering back can take many forms. At its simplest it might be a child on the telephone during a game show directing activities in a live studio broadcast. A notion much promoted during discussions on digital television, was that different endings to a film – or different branches throughout a story – could be offered, and the viewer would choose which branch they wanted to take. Voting and shopping through the television are obvious further uses, particularly since specialized shopping and holiday channels were early colonizers of satellite and cable television bandwidth.

More exciting, because more revolutionary in terms of traditional viewing habits, is the so-called convergence of TV with the Internet. Now, the likely extent of this convergence can be exaggerated, because watching and participating are two different activities. However there are large areas of over-lap, which are particularly exciting for producers of programming. Nearly every user of the Internet is waiting for more bandwidth. More bandwidth not only means stuff downloading more quickly to your computer – or TV, if that's how you're connected. It means bigger stuff downloading – stuff you wouldn't have attempted before, like decent quality video.

The whole point of the Internet is that any computer can talk to any other connected computer at any time. The music industry has already been changed by the Internet. There are bands who exist only through the Internet, because it allows them to by-pass the stranglehold that the record companies have on the means of distribution. Control the means of distribution and you control the industry – but no-one controls the Internet. Video on demand is a (limited) reality through the Internet, using broadband connections such as ADSL and the data channels on TV satellites. It will become an important sub-world for people who think of themselves primarily as film-makers or TV producers, because it puts power back in the hands of the creative individual. There are still problems of how to make money this way, and of advertising – you can have the best material in the world, but if no-one knows about it, it won't be any good to you or anyone else . . . None the less, the Internet is important as a means in itself, and as a warning to the old world.

Technology

This is a good place to consider changes in technology as an influence on the way the TV industry has changed, particularly as it affects independent programme-makers now.

In the beginning all TV was live. There are people who believe that the only true TV is live, and everything else is a regrettable fall from grace. Film could be shown on television, of course, and live television could be 'telerecorded'. Sounds grand, but telerecording was little more than a film camera pointing at a TV screen. The only record we have of TV before 1960 is from recordings made in this way.

Then, in 1956, Ampex demonstrated the first video tape recorder. The electronic age dawned. Programmes could now be recorded (editing was still a major problem), and even sold on tape to other broadcasters. As long as they used the same television standard. When colour TV came along the situation became even worse. The Americans developed colour TV first, with their 525 line, 60 fields a second system called NTSC (National Television Standards Committee). A basic problem with the NTSC standard was (and is) that it works fine under perfect conditions, but under real world conditions it tends to lose the ability to tell the difference between red and blue. British engineers called it Never Twice the Same Colour, in contrast to the European system, PAL, Peace (or Pictures) At Last. The PAL (Phase Alternating Line) system is basically a higher resolution (625 line, 50 cycles a second) sort of second generation version of NTSC that fixes the colour confusion problem. France, of course, invented its own system, SECAM (Sequential Couleur avec Memoir) which is superior and completely incompatible with anything else. It's therefore known as System Essentially Contrary to the

American Method, and, strangely enough, cannot be used inside studios, where PAL is used for working before transcoding to SECAM for distribution.

Standards convertors were slow to arrive, and it was even longer before they gave results that satisfied producers. The result that this had for international programming was that for a very long time, film remained the primary acquisition and production medium so that programmes which had international sales potential could be sold without too many problems.

The world of television was most definitely a studio-based world. Anything filmed outside involved a train of outside broadcast vehicles, or a film crew, both of which were seen as expensive and probably unnecessary. There's still a kind of folk-memory even now of outside scenes being expensive to shoot.

In 1971, Philips produced the first videocassette recorder. And Sony produced its competing Umatic videocassette format. Both were intended as domestic formats, but they were too big, heavy and expensive, and in fact, the spread of videocassettes into the home had to wait until the next generation, the VHS–Betamax wars. But by the mid 1970s, a combination of Sony's more reliable Umatic cassette format, and the appearance of lightweight electronic cameras led to the next revolution. The RCA TK76 was only lightweight compared to the studio cameras it was replacing, but it quickly became the mainstay of American news operations, and in 1977 the BBC began experiments in using similar lightweight (only about 35lb) cameras for electronic news gathering. It wasn't long before this equipment replaced film for news, then documentaries. But the savings were not always where people expected them. In terms of speed of getting pictures back for news, electronic acquisition has obvious advantages. In terms of picture quality, film was undeniably better. Even in terms of production costs, money goes in different places, but on all but the fastest lowest budget productions, tape was not necessarily the obvious choice over film. Apart from anything else, in the mid 1980s, we were still in a world where a studio VTR cost around £65,000, and a lightweight electronic camera around £35,000. A 16mm film camera on the other hand could be had for perhaps £12,000, and a Steenbeck for maybe £4000. (To put some kind of perspective on this, the house in a reasonably expensive part of England I bought in 1980 cost £27,000.) The prices of equipment kept production firmly in the hands of big companies.

As the independent production sector – and the use of videocassettes – developed during the 1980s, the electronic equivalent of the film service companies developed in the cities, usually rivalling the broadcasters for the level of equipment, and certainly for the speed with which it was operated. Clients didn't want to spend too much time waiting if they were editing in a suite costing them £350 an hour. What was possible, and the prices at which it was possible to achieve it, changed all the time, but the nature of the production industry remained broadly the same – until the digital revolution.

Digital technology first appeared in studio equipment in the mid 1970s, when an American company developed the first digital video effects (DVE) generator called 'SqueeZoom', because that's basically what it did. The BBC bought one and used it on their 6p.m. news programme *Nationwide*. Every time the pictures were switched through it, the quality dropped massively. But it could do live on-air things that had previously taken a week in a film laboratory to achieve. A British company, Quantel, produced a similar, but higher quality piece of equipment, which quickly spread throughout the PAL TV world.

The basic technology behind these DVEs was to store a single television frame digitally, after which you could manipulate it at will. In a far less spectacular way, digital frame-stores and time-base correctors (TBCs) became the mainstay of most studio and edit facilities.

But the frames were still stored or put through in uncompressed format, which uses a lot of memory, and a very high data rate. There was no way of handling and storing that amount of data in real time.

So the main development work of the digital revolution was in improving compression techniques. All the compression methods use similar techniques, some more efficiently than others: in a scene which consists basically of a talking head, very little changes in the picture between one frame and the next. So all you need to remember is the first frame of the scene, and throw away everything except the changes during the rest of the scene. The total amount of data that has to be stored is then much less.

Various acquisition formats are discussed later. What matters here is that suddenly, in around 1998, high quality equipment began to be available at prices small companies and even individuals could afford. You still needed the skills to operate the equipment, but if one result of the digital revolution was an enormous increase in the number of channels available to viewers, the other side was a democratization of the production process – in purely technical terms, at least.

Independent production

I've referred occasionally to the place of independent producers in the general scheme of things during the previous pages, but it's worth taking it as a separate subject.

The first thing to say is that the system did not have an acknowledged place for independent producers at all until the opening of Channel 4. But there *were* independent producers before then. Not many, but a few. Rather than work on programmes fully-commissioned, fully financed by the broadcasters, they tended to involve themselves with co-production, bringing together broadcasters from different countries to pay for a difficult or expensive programme.

The system didn't like it. The position from which all broadcasters started was 'We produce all our own programmes. Nobody tells us what to do.' In practice, this was never possible, but television programmers really didn't like admitting that they had to co-operate with others to get their programmes made, or to buy from others to fill their schedules.

But prices rise, and the world changes. During the 1960s and most of the 1970s, very little of this sort of thing went on. In the 1980s, however, the pace of change accelerated rapidly.

MIP TV is held every year in April in Cannes, and is arguably the single most important international television programme market of the year. In 1984 it was still largely visited by around 6000 buyers and sellers from broadcast television stations around the world. By 1999 there were nearly 17,000 registered delegates. Where do all the others come from? The new TV channels, of course, but mainly the independent production and distribution sector. That single statistic probably better explains the way the world has changed than any other.

Most people, whether broadcasters or producers, would rather work on their own and sell the finished product. Co-production is always a compromise. But it's about empowerment. During the 1980s, HTV became so frustrated with the domination of the ITV network by the big five that it started a campaign of co-production, producing a string of glossy, high production-value films and mini-series that it thought the network would find impossible to ignore. Without co-producing these programmes – with American TV, or Spanish, or French – HTV could not possibly have afforded them.

Unfortunately for everyone, they were (mostly) not very good. The gloss and the hype came before the script, and the result tended to be a collection of extremely pretty, but empty, boxes.

So HTV's exercise not only did not produce the desired effect – the access to the network that it wanted – it also produced an 'I told you so' atmosphere around co-production which still survives today. Co-production is very reluctantly entered into by TV stations.

When they do become involved in co-productions, many broadcasters still have at heart the attitude of the BBC at that time, where I actually had it said to me: 'This is a co-production. That means you give us the money, and we make the programme.'

Another anecdote: a very large Canadian animation company was in co-production discussions with the BBC during the late 80s, and was made a deal offer which really didn't make any sense from their point of view. 'Why should I do a deal like that?' asked the Canadian. The BBC were perplexed at this reaction, 'Why – the prestige.' they said.

The opening of Channel 4 was important to independent producers because it provided an outlet; a source of work, for them. But it was far more important as a catalyst. Suddenly an independent production sector was expected to exist. Suddenly broadcasters were wondering where all these producers were going to come from.

Another of the men who have shaped television in Britain: Jeremy Isaacs.

Jeremy Isaacs was the first Head of Programmes at Channel 4. As such he shaped the way the channel grew and was thought of. He was an extremely experienced and respected producer (*The World at War*), and so had the confidence to try out something very different when Channel 4 opened. The commissioning editors he hired were deliberately chosen to be *not* from the existing broadcasting establishment. Jeremy Isaacs wanted this channel to be different, and it wasn't going to be different if right from the start it was run by people who thought they knew what TV should be – or worse, thought they could do something new, but were unable to escape the chains of their own experience.

It was a brave experiment, and mainly successful. It has resulted in a unique culture at Channel 4, which produces some fascinating sights as it tries to be simultaneously a minority channel, and a commercial channel with appeal to Everyman of the twenty-first century.

At least Independent Producers were now acknowledged as animals, if not actually personae grata in the corridors of the Old Broadcasters. The publisher-broadcaster model of the licence renewals of 1992 theoretically gave a wider market to the indies. But in practice it didn't, as the companies bought each other up and Carlton, for instance, took over Central, and was able to produce all its own programmes in house, as Meridian and HTV and Anglia all joined together.

Thatcher's government did do one positive thing for independent producers, however, when it decided (as a way of increasing the competition they so loved) to require both the BBC and the ITV network to commission *at least* 25 per cent of its output from independent producers.

Independent production in Britain – indeed the whole of the film and television industry – exists entirely in a market-driven, market-commanded environment. There are positive and negative aspects to this, but whatever your position, it's interesting to note that the situation is quite different in most of Europe. If a producer in Germany, France, Austria, has an idea for a film or programme, very often the first question they ask themselves is not, 'Where can I sell this?' but 'Where can I go for a subsidy?' The culture of the European Community – as an organization, and in most of its member states, though not the UK – is to support what's technically known as the 'audiovisual' industry, in its widest sense. This, too, has both positive and negative sides, but it creates a distinct difference in approach to programming, and to the position of small producers in the world.

The launch of Channel 5 was greeted with some hope by independent producers in Britain. Unfortunately the hope was short-lived. United News and Media, which owned Anglia, Meridian, and HTV, also had a major stake in Channel 5. An announcement was made very early on that the channel was not to be thought of as a second Channel 4 in terms of opportunities for independent producers. Yes, they would be commissioning from independents, but only from an approved list of perhaps 30 companies. The other members of PACT, the Producers' Association could go jump . . .

This was a particular disappointment, partly because there were, by now, around 1200 members of PACT. Presumably any production company, large or small, which pays up to join PACT is serious about producing for television. Presumably, too, there were other companies and individuals who produced or intended to produce for TV, who were not members of PACT. So the independent production sector had grown from practically nothing in 1982, to represent a significant proportion of the whole industry by the mid 1990s – particularly when you consider what a small industry it is.

The marketplace

So, where are we now? We're in a world of television which, in terms of the way it commissions and produces programmes, is completely different from the world of the 'golden age' of the 1960s and 1970s. None the less, that image of how television works still informs the way we think about it – thinking still of BBC, ITV, and the rest. In particular, Channel 5 had not really impinged very much on the national consciousness by the end of the century.

Instead of two channels producing nearly everything for themselves, we have hundreds of channels, most of whom have to acquire – buy in – nearly all the programming they transmit. Increasingly, the medium is not important. You don't watch a programme because it's on satellite or digital terrestrial TV, you watch it because you want to see it. You don't buy into satellite or digital TV because of the technology, but because of the programming (normally sports or films in the case of the first decision to subscribe) that the technology offers. You are not connected to the Internet because you are able to dial into it with your computer, but because you want to achieve something when you're there – acquire knowledge, make friends with people on the other side of the world, chat with old friends, just look around.

Similarly you don't buy a book because it's book-shaped, or a magazine because of the binding, but because you're interested in what's between the covers. You don't buy a disc because it's a CD, or a DVD, but because of the music on it.

For a general interest channel like ITV or BBC1, this leads to lengthy debates, lots of navel-gazing, and lots of money spent (usually fruitlessly in the long run) on market-research, and focus groups. Most of the newer channels are much more tightly focused from a content point of view and so, while they obviously have to satisfy and enthuse their audiences, they don't have to attempt to please all of the people all of the time.

John Birt, in his farewell speech as Director General of the BBC, bemoaned the loss of 'community' that the arrival of the world of digital television had brought about. In the old days, when there was one channel, then everyone who watched TV at all watched the same thing and talked about it together in offices and pubs and homes afterwards. Even when there were four channels, this was still more or less the case. Obviously with hundreds of available choices, it's unlikely that your neighbours and colleagues will be watching the same things as you do.

But then they don't read the same newspapers or listen to the same music, either. This 'community' of viewers, through which the BBC held the entire nation together in a single happy family, was a very short-lived phenomenon, perhaps 20 years long, from the middle 1960s onward. Radio had perhaps had a similar binding effect in the previous 30 years, but the whole argument is a very BBC one. We have the multiplicity of channels that we do, not only because the technology is there, and the channels have been forced on an unwilling public who don't know better.

This is a commercial world. We have the multiplicity of channels because we want them.

The launch of digital terrestrial television in Germany, a couple of years before its launch in the UK, was a failure. Viewers weren't interested. BSB failed because there weren't enough viewers to make it work financially. Again, we don't buy technology, we buy content. Stories.

Producers in the multi-channel world

From our point of view as producers this multi-channel environment brings advantages and disadvantages in equal measure. The main and obvious advantage is that there are hundreds of new opportunities, hundreds of new places to sell our work – but, unfortunately, most of the channels have no money for original programming. There are more opportunities for people to work in the industry – but fewer long-term jobs for them.

The disadvantages are sometimes more subtle. I've already discussed how difficult it is now for newcomers to acquire a solid background of experience. It's also much harder to find an environment where ideas can grow, rather than being forced, and where long-term research – or filming – can happen. Certain kinds of programming are much harder to achieve in this new environment.

So how do we find ways around these shortages of time and money? The obvious solution is for us to make the programmes from our own resources; or finance them by pre-sales to two or three of these channels – and then to sell to as many of the others as we can.

And, increasingly, this is a world-wide market. Some programmes will only ever be of interest to a single country, or even region; but some can be sold all around the world, because the same situation is developing everywhere.

We are, all of us, working in a marketplace. We are in this business to make a living, not to make expensive home-movies. And our marketplace changed radically world-wide during the last few years of the twentieth century.

One of the things that happened is that the marketplace became a world-wide one. National, and then private television stations launched in countries all around the world – and the costs of providing programmes to fill all these hours of screen time never goes down. Television in small countries has to rely largely on imported programmes to fill its schedules, not because any country has a particular desire to watch the television of other countries, but because it simply can't afford to produce enough of its own.

There are two reasons why the world's television is full of American (and Australian) series: firstly because they come from societies which are (a) new, and (b) composed of a mixture of peoples and languages from many backgrounds, all of whom are seeking a common language with which to understand each other – even if only on a superficial level. The Hollywood silent movies achieved this brilliantly.

Secondly, there's just so much available, because the US market is big enough to provide for factory production methods. You want a daily soap – 365 episodes a year? Fine, we've got it. The size of the market and the sheer numbers sloshing around in their industries mean enormous catalogues available for sale, and vast quantities of wallpaper for impoverished television in other parts of the world. Although the workers of Los Angeles might like to believe otherwise, the whole world is not necessarily crying out to be more like them. But they do make good wallpaper.

Ideally, every country would have its own local programming, and be in a position to buy from other country's producers in order to improve their programme mix, and the interest of their schedule, rather than out of necessity to fill airtime.

And the paradox of local international programming is making this possible, to an extent. It's not actually that new. It was already being done back in the 1960s in limited ways, but there is a growing trend to produce different versions of the same programme for different markets. The multi-national Disney Channel, for instance, often produces the same show in different versions and different languages at the same time.

Power-shift

The balance of power in television is changing. The world where a powerful duopoly – or triumvirate – had absolute control over what we all saw is dying. It's much more useful to think of television programme making in terms of the paradigms of the Hollywood movie, for instance. Consider the cinema chains as the TV channels. They're the means of delivery of the product to the end-user. Not just in Hollywood, but everywhere, it isn't the cinemas that decide what films are made, it's the studios, the distributors, even the producers.

In book publishing, the book shops have no say in what books are written. The publishers make the decisions, and produce the books they consider they can sell.

Similarly in the 'new television', most new channels, most of the time, have to choose from what's available in the marketplace, rather than decide for themselves what they are going to do.

This means that the power of decision over who makes which programmes has shifted, and is continuing to shift from the broadcasters to the distributors. Media groups such as Pearson, News International, Bertelsmann, Kirch, Endemol already have more power than any broadcasters. But it's not all roses for the little people. Just as we've seen happen in the ITV system, that power is gradually becoming consolidated into a small number of ever larger groups.

However, it does mean that the little people have a much greater chance of somehow carving out their own niche in which to exist in this world. It's going to be the medium-sized companies that have the most trouble. If a small company produces one or two series a year, that can be quite a reasonably happy existence for the partners. A slightly larger company needs to turn over much more simply in order to pay for the greater overheads they have in terms of the office space and the staff they need just to be a slightly larger company.

So, in a nutshell, this is the situation we want to achieve: to produce a good programme, or preferably series, which can be shown on several different channels over time, which has been made very cost-effectively, so that we can make a profit sooner rather than later. The rest of this book is about some of the ways in which you can achieve that desirable situation.

TV in Britain – a brief timeline

1937 The BBC initiates one of the claimants to be the world's first commercial television service – which then closes at the start of the war in 1939.

1947 The BBC begins transmissions again – in 'high-definition' 405 lines black and white.

1955 ITV begins transmissions.
Reuters Television founded as BCINA

1964 BBC2 opens in 625 lines B/W.

1967 Regular colour transmissions begin.

1968 The first round of ITV licence renewals. Changes include the creation of Thames Television out of a forced marriage between ABC and Associated Rediffusion; and the birth of London Weekend TV.

1977 Annan Report recommends a fourth channel.

1980 Second round of ITV licence renewals. Southern loses to TVS.

1982 Opening of Channel 4.
Sky Television begins transmissions to cable stations.

1986   British Sky Broadcasting begins transmissions.

1990   Sky takes over BSB to form BSkyB.

1992   ITV licences renewed by auction. Publisher-broadcasters appear: Carlton, Meridian, a re-modelled HTV.

1997   Channel 5 begins broadcasting.

1998   Sky begins a digital service.

1999   OnDigital, digital terrestrial television, begins in Britain.

PUTTING THE PROGRAMME TOGETHER

Having the right idea

Before you make a programme, you have to know what it's going to be. Obvious? Perhaps. None the less it's a statement worth making. You want to make programmes, make films, don't you? Do you have a burning desire to make one particular film at this moment? Maybe you have. But we all have to make a living. It won't stop there. We hope.

Just as a furniture maker has to decide first of all which particular shape to turn his or her skills to for the next piece of work, so do we all. Our skills are in telling stories on the screen. I believe that's true whatever form we choose to take – whether it's big-screen fiction, small screen docu-soap, or anything in between.

Ultimately whatever we do is story-telling. Even an atmospheric portrait of a person, place, or group of people is a story. And if it isn't, then you'll lose your audience long before the end. That isn't to say that what you do has to follow traditional nursery-school narrative forms. But I believe that no linear presentation can exist without a narrative thread of some kind, however well concealed. And linear presentation is what we do, isn't it? We start somewhere – at a place of our choosing; and we take an audience on a journey to somewhere else, in the hope of enriching and entertaining them on the way.

Even so-called 'non-linear' media are essentially composed of a number of small linear elements. The difference is that the order in which these elements are viewed is under the control of the viewer, not the producer.

So we're going to make a film (I use the word generically). What is it going to be? We can talk about which camera to use, what angles, how many crew all day long – but, ultimately (well, not ultimately; in the first place) the camera has to be pointing at something. What is it pointing at, and why?

There are basically two ways to make the decision. You make it. Or it's made for you. Of course it's rarely quite that clear cut, but ultimately, either you decide for yourself what you're going to do, do it, and sell it; or a broadcaster needs a certain programme, and they commission you to provide it to them.

Deciding on a project to develop will mean rejecting a lot of ideas. Be tough on yourself, because, however hard you are, it's going to be the friendliest reaction you get. We'll look at the technical and financial constraints on what you can do later on. In terms of the market, and in the context of making a living, here are a few things to consider:

Pitching

If you are pitching to a single channel, look at their current schedule. Look at the way their transmission slots are organized. It may change, but in general, channels need to present a recognizable face to viewers. Viewers need to know what to expect when they turn to that channel at that time of the day and week. So it's unlikely that a channel is going to change its face completely.

Once you've done that, you're able to suggest, as part of your pitch, a suitable slot for your idea. If they have never run 10 minute episodes of anything, then it's going to be a hard sell to persuade them to take your 10 minute programmes. Much better to fit your programme to the character and slot length of the channel as it is. That way, the buyer or commissioner doesn't have to work too hard to say 'yes'. Increasingly, we live in a world where people prefer to say 'no', because it's easier. Brave and imaginative decisions *are* made in television – occasionally, but it's long been very hard to find people with both the power and the will to use that power to say 'I believe in this idea. Let's do it.'

Single programmes are a very hard sell. Everyone wants series because they fill the schedule easily, meaning that a single purchasing or scheduling decision can take care of a lot of problem at one go; and because a series builds an audience. A single show has to be sold to the audience, too – and then a whole new sell has to start the following week in that slot. In practice, most single films that are shown, are shown within some kind of umbrella slot. In *Shark Week*, on Discovery Channel, for instance, the programmes come from several different sources. The 'season' is not a homogenous production.

If you must make a single film, then try either to package it with others, or at least suggest to the programme buyer how it might fit with others in their schedule to form a themed package.

Television intended for international sale has to be of some kind of interest to people in other countries. The most unlikely stories can travel. But it's unlikely that a factual series about traffic wardens in a provincial British city is going to be seen very much outside the UK. (I'm no doubt wrong about that particular instance, but I'm sure you get the point.)

There's no single right answer. Every programme is a prototype, and we all hope to be making different programmes for different markets. But it's only sensible to be sure that you're developing round pegs for round holes, and hexagonal pegs for hexagonal holes. At least that way you start with a reasonable chance.

Forced choices

This kind of extremely efficient programme-making does make certain choices for you. In a nutshell, you either have to work very quickly, or you work alone.

Programmes that require lots of time are going to be very difficult, if not impossible, to do within the available budget: for example observational documentaries following events as they unfold over weeks or months; wildlife productions which involve a lot of time spent waiting for something to happen. This kind of thing tends to be either very expensive, or done by one-person teams.

It goes without saying that you're unlikely to be able to do anything involving big casts or big stars – although you might be able to stage your scene in front of an event involving large crowds that's happening anyway. Why fill Trafalgar Square with New Year's Eve revellers when you can take your two actors along and get them to do their scene in front of the real thing for next to nothing?

And programmes involving lots of travel are difficult, because travel is expensive and time-consuming. Although there are ways around this, too.

The clever thing to do is to fit the project to your resources, so that you can make everything work really well, rather than to try to achieve something you know in your heart of hearts isn't really going to work. Think before you spend.

BUDGETS AND COSTING

Film and television programming is expensive. There's no way round it. Even producing programmes as efficiently as possible for amounts of money that would have been thought risibly small only a few years ago, the sums are still too large for most people to command on their own – even if it were sensible so to do.

First of all, there's no excuse for going over budget. Earthquake, wars, nuclear explosion, maybe. Otherwise, nothing. If you go over budget, either the show was budgeted unrealistically in the first place, or you lost track of it during the production process. Neither of these is excusable. The only important rule of budget control is: either have enough money to do what you want to do; or make sure that what you are doing will be possible within the resources you have. In practice, it's a continual juggling act, but in essence it's quite simple.

Because the sums involved are large, there's a tendency for people – particularly those on the periphery – to think that there's more money available than there is. If a film or series is sensibly budgeted, even if it costs £10 million, there won't be enough money to give away the odd few thousand to someone extra who feels they deserve a fee. 'A film is like a sow,' someone once said to me, 'as soon as it shows up, people fasten on to it and try to suck money out.'

At the very tightly controlled budget levels we're dealing with here, there's certainly no chance of losing the odd unexpected payment. Even so, you'll find that you might still be dealing with budgets heading well towards the millions – it's just that conventionally you'd expect the amounts to be many times more.

We're currently engaged on a 3D computer animation project, whose costs work out at around just under £4000 per minute. It's less than half the price you might expect to pay. Even so, for the 39 × 7 minutes (to make 13 half-hours) the total budget is nearly £1 million. And there's very little spare in that figure, large though it might seem.

Just as a story can be told in any number of ways, so there's no single 'right' budget for a programme. Different ways of telling your story will obviously have different cost implications. You can't say (as some people try to) that a minute of documentary television must cost, say, £2500, or a minute of drama or animation costs £10,000. It all depends on how *you* are going to do it.

However, you can probably take those figures as very rough guides for the way things tend to work out if you use standard ways of thinking. If you're reading this book, you probably want to spend less. 'Industry-standard' ways of approaching production and costing tend to mean that budgets will find a 'natural' industry-standard level. I'm not proposing a totally different way of making a programme. It's important to be clear that this is about being extremely efficient in the use of more or less traditional resources. It's about not being lazy in using money as a substitute for thought. You have to get it right first time. And if you only need a two-man crew, then use a two-man crew. On the other hand if you really do need a crew of twenty-five, then don't try to do the job with two.

In *Day for Night* Truffaut says that making a movie is a bit like going on a stage-coach journey in the Old (wild) West. When you start out, you hope for a good journey. After a while, you just hope you'll get there in one piece. He's right. But a lot of pain can be prevented by thinking things through clearly – and honestly – early on. Again, if you find you really can't find a way of getting

(a)

(b)

Figure 3.1 Low budget doesn't have to mean one-man bands. *The Chef's Apprentice* at Hever Castle (a) and Longleat House (b).

the budget below £100,000, then don't fool yourself into thinking that somehow it'll work out going ahead with £60,000. It won't come out in the wash. It won't be alright on the night.

Paper is cheap. And time spent early on in the planning stage is cheap, too. You may find you have to re-think the whole project two or three times. The time to do that is when only you and maybe one or two others are involved. Not when you have a crew of thirty and a helicopter all waiting for something to happen at a combined cost of £2000 per hour. You can't stop the meter running while you work out what went wrong at that stage.

Budget forms

Some people are frightened of budget forms. There's no need to be. All they are is shopping lists. Actually, 90 per cent of making a movie is shopping lists. A feature film budget book is intimidating, but only because the list is so long. There's no point in using it for a simple documentary, because half of the items on it don't apply. In any case, you don't have to put a number by every line. The list is there to make sure that you consider every line, but if you don't need something, then don't have it.

All you need is this really, really short list. It has three items on it:

1 **What are we filming?**
That is to say, what's the action, and who is performing – cast, interviewees, audience, the question is the same.
2 **Who is filming it?**
Have we got a crew, and what equipment do they need?
3 **Where are we filming?**
Is the location agreed, paid for if necessary – is it organized and suitable?

That's it. Just go round and round those three items again and again from the first day of planning to the last day of filming.

Computers are very useful, because they do sums for you. I use two basic budget forms, with variations for studio shows, or film: a long one for drama, and a short one for factual programmes. They're line-by-line spreadsheet extracts from the standard 'books' that broadcasters such as Channel 4 use, so anyone looking through them should recognize the blocks into which the budget decisions fall.

Doing the budget

A budget never actually stands still, because things change all the time. However, there are roughly three broad phases in production budgeting: the preliminary budget, the working budget, and then the budget-tracking phase.

The preliminary budget is a reasonably sensible cost for the series. It will be as accurate as you can make it with the information you have available at the time. You probably don't know yet exactly where something will be filmed, or who the cast is going to be, or the presenter (if you have them).

The final budget is the budget agreed by everyone involved in the production (including financiers and commissioning editors) before you go into production. You should know by now exactly how many nights in hotels you're going to have to pay, and what the fees of your talent are going to amount to.

Finally, as the production progresses, tracking the budget closely means that you know that if you spend less in one area, you have enough to cope with an under-estimate in another. All budgets should have this kind of built-in contingency, so that if you don't need the helicopter after all, then the unexpected contribution to the church bell fund won't change the overall spend on the programme.

Before you begin, be aware of (roughly) what kind of figure you want to end up with. If you go blindly through filling in the form in a standard way, then you'll get a standard result. If there's nothing particularly special about the programme, a budget for a half-hour documentary filmed close to your base is always going to come out the same. If you need to make it on 35 mm film, then it will cost more. If, on the other hand, you need to make it for as little as absolutely possible, then I'd suggest you really start with a blank form. Don't edit something you've done before. Start from a desk and a telephone, think through the process of making the programme, and put into the budget only what you really need. It can be a very interesting process. Something which 'always' comes out at £200,000 can actually come down to a quarter of that in some cases.

But do be very sure that you do put in everything that you need. Don't fool yourself. It can only go horribly wrong if you do.

The line: above and below

Movie budgets are traditionally divided into two: above and below the so-called 'line'. Above the line are costs which can vary tremendously depending on who's doing the job: producer, director, writer, principal cast. The 'talent', if you like. Below the line are the budget elements which are more predictable: the crew, equipment, facilities, catering costs, so-called 'other' cast and extras. There tend to be going rates for this kind of thing, so the overall cost to the programme depends not so much on who or what they are, but how many (or much) there is.

An unknown actor may cost you the union minimum of around £800 for a week's work, for instance; but a star will demand what she or he thinks they're worth to the programme. The name brings the audience. Marlon Brando was reputedly paid over $1 million for his day's work on the first *Superman* film. We're not in that game, here, but you may find that somehow finding the extra money for some kind of a 'name' participant can make the difference between whether the project makes it to the screen or not.

Budgeting, scheduling, and the way you decide to do the programme are so intricately entwined that it's difficult to separate them. I'm going to try, but I'm aware that some of these decisions are recursive: if you decide to shoot in five days instead of ten, obviously your crew costs are going to be lower. Whether you make that decision in order to fit in with a fixed amount of available finance, or from a belief that that's really all you need makes a difference to the whole shape of the budget.

Development

'Development' is the phase of programme-making that leads up to the formal beginning of pre-production. It's usually the longest phase, and the least well costed. The true cost of development includes all the time you spent between productions trying to get the next one financed. All the other projects that never got anywhere; all the lunches you bought for commissioning editors and financiers; all those taxis between meetings. The drinks you bought while 'networking' at the Groucho Club; the fluffy pen-tops with the company logo that you sent out with the Christmas cards. The Christmas cards. And so on.

All of this belongs to the true cost of running a production company – even of being a freelance producer – and has to be accounted for and recognized when you work out how much profit you've made. However, you can only charge to a production budget the direct development costs associated with that production. A proportion of the rest can be included at the end of the budget as 'company overheads', but really, you just have to accept that a successful production pays for all the others, and not try to account for all that wasted time. Just don't pretend that it never existed.

This isn't about how to run a company, but it *is* about making a living. The same rules apply in controlling company overhead costs as in a production budget. There's no point in making healthy profits on a production, only to find it disappears into paying the rent or the receptionist's salary, or for the company cars. Buy what you need when you need it. Then don't try to manage without.

Direct development costs can still be surprising. I'm not going to go through a whole budget form line by line, but it's worth looking at some of the things that can get away if you don't pay attention:

Options

If you have to acquire rights in a book – whether for a drama or a factual programme – then the option payments will be part of the cost of development. You had to pay them anyway, whether or not the film was made. That's an easy one, because you'll remember paying the money out.

Conventionally, you would expect to pay around 2 per cent of the budget for screen rights in a book – say, £20,000 for a film budgeted at £1 million. Option payments would be 10 per cent of the purchase price per year – £2000 in this case. That's a lot of money if we're trying to make programmes for as little outlay as possible. There are ways round it.

First of all, if you can't afford to play big boys' games, then stay out of the playground. There's no point in going for a top-ten best-selling novel, because you won't be able to afford it. In my experience, rights owners in the United States tend to demand enormous amounts for options – partly because they know that that's quite likely the only money they'll see. Studios have a habit of buying up options – or even buying rights outright – and never making the film.

It can still be worth buying the rights to a book, because the very fact that the story has already been published and achieved a certain success gives comfort to timid financiers that they are indeed getting involved in something worthwhile – someone else has already decided that the idea is worth investing in.

With properties with a lower profile, you can often do more sensible deals with publishers and agents. For instance, you could offer a very low option payment for six months, to be renewed at a higher rate if you were making progress on finding finance.

Or you could offer a higher than usual profit participation. The author of the book tends to receive about 2.5 per cent of the net profit. You could offer 5 per cent in return for lower option payments.

Some authors can be involved in the production itself, and this, too, can be a way of easing your cash-flow. You could guarantee a certain level of employment on the production in exchange for a lower option payment. Or you could simply offer a larger than usual sum to purchase the rights, but pay less now.

The idea behind all of these notions is to ease your cash flow by reducing payments out when there's nothing coming in.

Script development

You may have prepared a full script, or may only have needed a proposal document. Either way, the cost of preparing it should be charged to the production. Even if you did it all yourself.

In the real world, functions very often overlap, but it's unrealistic (and dangerous) to cut down on *budgeted* costs by assuming you'll be doing it all yourself, and charging the programme only half what it would cost if someone else did the job. That isn't fair to you, and, apart from anything else, what happens if you're unable to do it in the end (perhaps because another film comes along which has to be done at the same time) and you have to hire someone else to do it for you? You're over budget before you start, that's what happens. The only way to produce an honest preliminary budget is to charge for everything. If you are able to combine functions and do deals on fees in the event, then that's great. You come in under budget, which everyone loves. If you do it the other way round – cutting too many corners at the beginning, and finding you were wrong – you come in with massive overspends. And nobody is happy. *Even if the final figure ends up the same.* If your budget says the series will cost £100,000 and it costs £95,000 in the end, you're a hero. If you tell everyone it's going to be £90,000 and it turns out to be £95,000 you're incompetent, and unloved. Which would you rather?

Travel

You've almost certainly spent something on travel – going to pitch the project to co-producers or commissioning editors – even if it's only local rail fares. You're unlikely to forget if you've crossed the Atlantic to raise money – but even taxi fares count. If you don't know what the programme has truly cost, how will you know if you've made a profit?

Artwork costs

You may have commissioned an artist to do pictures for the proposal.

Pilot

Animation is very often bought on the basis of a 30 second pilot so show the quality of the pictures and animation. This is obviously a development cost.

Legal fees

If you've bought an option, or had contracts drawn up for finance, you'll have given money to lawyers. This is something that, once started, never ends.

Consultancy fees

This is a catch-all phrase, but you may well have paid someone to give advice, or make introductions on your behalf.

Research

Certainly you will have spent time on research. You may have paid fees to libraries, or interviewees. You will have spent money on telephone calls and photocopies.

Producer

And don't forget your own time – even if you decide to roll it into your company's general overheads, you shouldn't be working for nothing. If you want to take your digital camera out on the road, do your own filming and editing, that's fine; but it isn't what we're talking about here. This is about making a proper business out of television production.

Repayment

Particularly if you've persuaded an outside investor to put some money into the development of your project, it's conventional to repay the investment on the first day of principal photography.

Producers

How many producers do you need? On the one hand, in factual programming, the BBC, for example, make no distinction between producers and directors. In fact, increasingly, one person will do most of the research, set everything up, and direct the filming. Which makes sense in the kind of programme which is basically journalism-based. The producer is a journalist telling a story.

On the other hand, a large international co-production might have four or five executive producers, a producer, even a line producer, an associate producer, and then a director, as well. What do all these people do? They increase the size of the budget. But that isn't necessarily a bad thing, because some of them are there to look after the money they've brought to the project. Executive producers are normally financiers or repre-sentatives of the co-producers who make it possible for the programme to be made. Although they will often form a kind of committee with rights of approval, they tend not to be active in any day-to-day sense. If you co-produce a series with broadcasters from two different countries and a distributor, each partner will quite likely want at least a notional creative input, and their executive producer will be the person responsible for that. It can be a nightmare, or it can work well. My advice would be to keep it small, and try to work with people you know that you can work with on a personal level. That way the decision-making process is much faster and less painful.

The programme producer is the real overall leader of the creative team. The producer may or may not direct, but will have brought together the writer(s), cast, and director, and will manage the day-to-day running of the production, and tell the director that she or he can't have the things that it's the director's job to ask for. Control of the budget is ultimately the producer's responsibility.

Line producers are a kind of half-way stage between a production manager and the programme producer. You'd normally only expect to find them on large and/or long-running programmes.

Associate producer? That's another job that means what you want it to mean. Some broadcasters have a formal job called 'associate producer' – a kind of assistant producer only not really an assistant. More often it tends to be a way of rewarding people who have done something to get the programme off the ground, but who can't be given a job with real responsibility or decision-making power. An example might be a writer who came up with the original idea, and who wants involvement in the production process, but has no real experience of production. They can still be useful as a part of the team, but you wouldn't want them to run it.

And the director? The director is the person directly responsible for what appears on the screen, using the resources that the producer will have assembled for him or her.

If the executive producer provides the cash; the producer spends it on assembling a team with a script in the right place at the right time; the director makes sure that something useful is going on there, and that the camera is pointing at it.

Normally in our kind of programme-making, the producer and director will be the same person – maybe you. But here, as everywhere else, bringing in a project at the lowest possible budget level doesn't mean spending as little as you can get away with on absolutely everything. Particularly when you're trying to use every resource in the most efficient way possible, directing is an immensely technical, nuts and bolts job. There's no time to keep getting it wrong and changing your mind. Or for shooting miles more than you need. If you can do it, that's wonderful, but in the end, it's the director who will make these cost-efficient methods work – or not. If you can do it yourself, that's brilliant. If you can't, then don't try – or at least don't try when it really matters. Of course everyone has to learn somehow, but not everyone has to learn firefighting on a burning oil rig. You can start on bonfires and work up.

There's no mystery about directing; but efficient programme-making is not possible with an inefficient director.

So, beware the number of producers . . . and make sure you have (or are) a good director.

Crew

We'll look at crewing in more detail later. The most important thing is to be sure that you have the right number of people. The list is long, but you don't need everyone on it. On the other hand, if you cut it down too much, you'll find that doesn't work, either.

There is a lot that can be done with a two-person crew, camera and sound; but I've often found it quicker to have a third person. The daily cost is higher, but you get more done. At the very least, it's someone to help carry gear from one place to another. If the third person is a qualified electrician they can often pre-light the next location, saving a crucial 20 or 30 minutes. Two of those a day can make a big difference.

And that brings us on to the real budget-destroyer, overtime. Don't be naive about overtime. It's surprising how quickly an 8 hour day disappears – particularly when the crew include travelling time to the location. It's usual to do deals with people for a 10 hour day or, if possible, an overall all-in fee, with overtime included. Most people will only do a deal like that if they trust you not to ask them to work all night, and who can blame them? You may find that electricians are reluctant to do any deals at all.

Be sensible about overtime. First of all, people are happier, more efficient, and make better decisions if they haven't been working all night. Secondly, working long hours often doesn't save money. Apart from the progressive drop in efficiency, the sum is quite simple: if you're paying £100 an hour, a day costs £800. A 12 hour day costs £1400, because the last 4 hours are at time and a half. For the price of three 12-hour days (£4200 and 36 hours), you can have more than five normal days (42 hours). That's nearly a whole day's working time thrown away. Naturally this assumes that there isn't a problem with deadlines. Personally I used to work long hours and do shoots into the evening and edits past midnight, but I don't any more. Because there isn't any need. Don't be taken in by the hype of those people who don't feel they're making real television unless they've been up all night. The work isn't good. People aren't happy. The budget is often shot to pieces.

Whatever you do, do all the deals, and make sure everyone is happy *before you start*. Producers who try to do deals on overtime afterwards, when people have worked long hours, and are owed lots of money become very unpopular very quickly. How would you like it if you'd just worked a 60 hour week, and were due a couple of thousand pounds extra, and the producer came along and asked if you could possibly accept £200? Or kind of, forget the overtime altogether . . .?

Of course you need stamina. Of course you should be prepared to work long hours if necessary. But don't do it unless it really is necessary, because it doesn't get the job done efficiently.

Here, as everywhere else in the preliminary budget, it's better to round things up, rather than down. Don't budget for big discounts or deals yet. That way you end up with a bottom line that shows the worst case, rather than something that's over-optimistic. And you have a more flexible budget with a number of in-built contingencies.

Cast

Ideally you'll produce separate budget forms for drama, entertainment, documentary programmes, but every kind of programme has some kind of cast.

If you have a presenter, consider how much you need to pay – and how many days you need them. Very often, all the presenter's filming can be compressed into a short time – maybe only a single day. Although presenters are often paid per programme, rather than per day, obviously the time taken is going to influence the fee that they demand.

If you're interviewing people in a documentary, are you going to pay the interviewees a fee? Or expenses? Conventionally you wouldn't expect to pay interviewees – but if you really need them for your programme, and they demand a fee, what are you going to do?

With a bit of luck you can sometimes get a big name actor or presenter by making an offer that runs something like: 'This is a really nice project; it's not going to take very much of your time; and we'll give you £2000 (or whatever). Of course you normally get more, but it's £2000 you wouldn't otherwise have, and it'll be fun. Take it or leave it.' Quite often they take it.

Music

Music is expensive. There'll be more about music, because it's a powerful piece of any programme, and often forgotten until too late, when you discover that you can't afford it. There are also some common misconceptions about what you can and cannot do with music.

The basic decision is whether to use library music, specially composed for film and television use, but which anyone can use; or whether to commission specially-composed music for your programme. Library music is generally cheaper if you're not using much – but since you pay a minimum of 30 seconds royalty for each separate music cue, it can quickly become more expensive than commissioning your own. As any composer will tell you.

Don't forget, too, that (unless you are making a series fully commissioned by a UK broadcaster) you should really be paying for world rights in all media, which is considerably more expensive than rights for UK broadcast only.

Stock

A fundamental decision to be made is whether you're going to shoot on tape or film. Except at the very lowest levels of budget, there's often less difference between the two than you might expect.

Because of the high cost of buying and processing film stock, shooting ratios are much more influential on the overall budget cost in film than in tape, where the stock itself is cheap.

However, someone is going to have to sort out all that footage sometime. If you let the camera run all day on location, then it's going to take much longer to find things in the edit. The money just goes in different places.

Whatever you do, don't take chances with stock. I would never use second-hand stock. I don't even re-use my own tapes, except perhaps for working or duplicating copies. It's foolish to risk throwing away a morning's work because you saved £10 on a roll of stock that turned out to be damaged, or full of dropouts. If it's suspect, bin it.

Kit

Choice of kit is something we'll come on to. Reliability is a big issue here, too. Cheap is not necessarily good. If you're filming overseas with a local crew, do you use their equipment, or do you bring your own camera, because you know you can trust it? There's no easy answer, but the question needs to be asked.

Think of paying more than the absolute minimum as a kind of insurance. It's certainly going to be cheaper and less painful to get the pictures first time than it is to go through a re-shoot, even if the insurance company does pay for it.

Travel and subsistence

And here's the second area, after overtime, where any budget can so quickly end up in tatters. Even if everyone involved in the programme travels from home every day and you only have to feed them at mid-day, the costs of travel and subsistence are always surprising.

If the programme requires overseas travel and overnights for crew and cast, then it can quickly add up to a major proportion of the budget – easily 10 per cent. It's one of the elements that tends to be forgotten when rough budgets are drawn up. 'Producer, director, script, crew, edit – that's not so bad . . .' But it's the ancillary costs that break a back-of-the-envelope budget like that one.

Financial costs

Even small productions should be properly insured. You may decide that you don't need to cover yourself against bad weather, but you certainly need to insure against something happening to the film or tape after the shoot. A rule of thumb is to allow 2 per cent of the budget, and in fact you'll normally find that it costs less in the event. If you have a reasonably regular flow of production through the year, it will be cheaper to take out an annual blanket insurance policy which will be valid for all production up to a certain cost.

On all but the simplest productions there'll be contracts involved – for finance, for delivery of the programmes, for engaging the crew and cast. Unfortunately legal advice does not come free.

There may be costs in financing the programme. If you're lucky, you may persuade buyers to pay something on the first day of principal photography, and the rest on completion. More likely, you won't be paid until you deliver. If the production period is short, that is not necessarily a problem. Otherwise, you'll have to find another way of cash-flowing the production. The ITV network, for instance, pays well, but only on delivery. It's up to the production company to find a bank to discount the contract you have with ITV – to lend you the money until you're paid. The interest you pay on borrowing the money is part of the overall cost of production.

Finally, it's conventional to add a general contingency of 10 per cent to the total to give you some room for mistakes – things which cost more than you expected, or take longer. Broadcasters who are fully-commissioning programmes often won't allow this kind of general contingency; but if you're sensible, there will already be little pockets of contingency hidden within the budget, so in any event you shouldn't count on having to spend this money – but, equally, you shouldn't count on pocketing it, either.

Case history: *Cookery Clinic*

It's easy to see why programme-making is such an expensive activity, but it's not so hard to keep control of it all. In the end it's just a shopping list.

We made a series called *Cookery Clinic* for a cable and satellite (cabsat) channel. It was a lively, Saturday-morning show. The pitch went something like: 'There are lots of programmes that show you how to amaze your friends and conjure up something wonderful in ten minutes – but there's nothing that tells you what to do when it all goes horribly wrong ...'

We were commissioned to produce a series of eight 47-minute programmes, with a total budget *for the series* of £50,000. In this case we knew that that was it. We would have £50,000. If we produced the eight hours for less, then we kept the change. If it cost more, we would have to pay the extra. Which is, of course, something we didn't want to do.

Figure 3.2 Recording *Cookery Clinic*. Cameramen in chef's whites so that they could work in shot.

So, in this case the problem clearly was to work out how to give as much quality as we could with the cash available – rather than to decide what we would ideally like to do, and then find out what it would cost.

This kind of computation is always a little bit circular. You say 'I'd like to do this or that . . . Can we afford it?' and then add bits and take away bits until you end up with some sums that work out.

We made a number of key decisions very quickly. The shows would be recorded 'as-live': that is, we would use three or four cameras going through a vision mixer as if we were doing a live broadcast. It would have been theoretically possible to do the whole thing with one camera, but that would have involved a lot of editing, and, more important for this kind of show, a lot of repetition, which would have made it difficult to produce the kind of atmosphere we wanted – particularly since we had also decided to do the show with an audience, who would be bringing their cookery problems with them.

The other real option was to record the output of three cameras separately and edit later, but that, too seemed unnecessarily long-winded – and would have been more expensive in the end.

Each programme would have a 'film' insert – a magazine-type story to help open the show out, and get us out of the studio.

Actually we also made the decision not to do the programme in a studio, but to use a real restaurant and build a temporary kitchen in the room where we did the recording. Not only was it slightly cheaper than using a studio – since we didn't have to build a full set – but it also looked more interesting.

We would record two shows a day, one in the morning, one in the afternoon.

Costing it

Beginning with only a desk and a telephone has advantages, in that you're not forced to work in a particular kind of way, or use a certain piece of equipment just because you own it. You can choose the best tools for the job. The disadvantage is that the only programme costs you have any control over are your own, which doesn't account for much of the budget.

We were able to find a location which wasn't going to cost us anything except whatever it took to put a 'kitchen' in the room, so the biggest cost was going to be the outside broadcast unit – people and equipment.

I've always found that the best way to hire crew and facilities is in a kind of pyramid. If I'm directing, it's important to me who the lighting cameraperson is, but (assuming they're a relatively normal human being) more important to me that the camera assistant gets on with the cameraperson, than that I choose them. So I pay the bills, but leave the chore of finding assistants to the head of department. In the same way, we found an outside broadcast facility company who trusted us to do what we said we would, and left booking the crew to them – although we did know a lot of the people anyway, and requested that certain key people be booked on our behalf. We did a fixed price deal with them to provide crew and equipment for the four recording days for a total of £28,000.

I have directed multi-camera, but it's not one of my strengths, so I engaged a director with whom I've often worked to do that for me. It was very important that that was well done, because it was soon clear that the only way to achieve the kind of quality we really wanted was by not doing any editing at all. That is to say, at the end of each day, we had to have two programmes which ran for exactly 47 minutes each. Luckily we had a crew and a director who loved live television.

The eight (five-minute) inserts were filmed in two days, all in London, and edited and finished before the recording days, so that they could simply be copied in to the final programme as we reached that point in the recording – and the audience could see them at the same time.

That accounts for the major budget items – crew and post-production: the crew were a fixed cost; and (apart from editing the inserts) there wouldn't be any post-production. Admittedly that's rare, but it was our particular solution to a budgeting problem. But beware. It's often the 'little' costs that conspire to ruin your over-optimistic budget.

Why do people usually go over budget? Either because things take longer than planned, so people have to be paid more; or because other items cost more than you thought. In this case the first problem was solved by having a fixed-price crew – although that's something you can only do if people trust you to deliver the working times you say you will. If you agree a ten-hour day and actually work 18 hours, obviously people are going to be reluctant to do a similar deal a second time.

What remained for us was all the other costs – which are *always* more than you think. I still think the cost of the woodwork for our temporary kitchen was high; and I think that's because in the end the people who did it were kitchen people, not TV people, and thought to themselves 'Aha! TV. Lots of money.' But it came within the overall budget. The other thing is the cost of food on a food programme. You have to have at least three times more than you need to allow for repetition; and you need a surprising amount for eight programmes. The point is, though, that all the surprises were at the beginning, when we were fitting things in to the budget. Not at the end, when all the money was spent.

Finally, music. More on music later. For *Cookery Clinic* we commissioned a theme tune, so that cost, too, was known.

You might have done things differently in a similar situation. There's never a single best way. The point is that we spent time on working out a way in which we were comfortable that we could reliably provide the best possible quality in the most efficient way. We found a way that we were confident would work – and it did. Of course there were a few little surprises, but they weren't, so to speak, unexpected surprises, and were contained within the overall budget figure.

The £50k movie

Cookery Clinic was produced in a slightly unusual way. Here's another example of first-principles costing to ponder on: the £50,000 movie.

There are sensible reasons why a reasonably standard two-hour drama costs something like $2 million. You'll find a standard budget for such a production in the appendix, and we've already discussed much of what makes up this total.

So let's throw it all out of the window and start again. We've got a producer (you), a desk, a telephone, and a book full of contacts. What do you really need to make a TV movie for a two-hour slot?

It's surprising how circumscribed your thinking can be without you even realizing it. Colleagues and I had several times tried this exercise – how little money it really took to make a movie – and had always come out with the same kind of number. First it was £300,000; then as low as £150,000. You have to be tougher on yourself and really think differently.

The basic question is what do I really really need to make a movie? You need a script; some actors; a camera person; a sound recordist; an editor – together with various bits and pieces of equipment. The reason that feature films have much bigger crews is partly because they have big stories requiring lots of people to get the whole process moving; but it's also partly habit.

Imagine a scene between two people – just dialogue – taking place in a small room. Even if you have a crew of 100 and a cast to match, the scene in the room is going to involve only six people, including the cast. The rest are going to wait outside because there's no room for them. So why do you need everyone else?

You normally do need a few more people in fact, but the trick is to be absolutely sure that you only have what you need – and that you do have what you do need.

Step by step

❑ First of all you find a story that requires only a small cast and a limited number of locations. The whole story doesn't have to take place in two rooms – this is a visual medium – but we can't go from Alaska to the Sahara, either. You pay a script fee equal to the Writers' Guild minimum for that kind of script.

❏ You pay your cast the minimum rates – but not less. And you don't forget that you'll need at least some walk-ons and extras.

So now you know what the action is, who's performing, and where it's happening (our basic shopping list). Now we need someone to shoot it.

❏ I suggest that your necessary crew is a basic three-person documentary crew: camera, sound, electrician. However big the crew, the real work is always done by those three people in the end, anyway. Everyone else supports them.

❏ Additionally you'll need a couple of runners to run, fetch and carry to support the camera crew and the production crew.

❏ Production staff? You, the producer, of course. The director; and a production assistant/continuity person who will also help with general production management. You can cut this differently: there may be a producer/director, but then I think you need another 'senior' production manager/line producer to allow the producer to be in two places at once. Because you need to be able to work very efficiently.

❏ Schedule? Ten minutes of finished screen time a day for ten days. It's a lot, but not unusual. Single-camera television drama expects 5 minutes a day in the UK, anyway, and series in the USA are often scheduled at 10 minutes a day.

❏ Since this is television, you shoot on tape – but not on cheap cameras unless you really want it to look like it was shot on cheap cameras.

❏ And finally you need to edit, so you need the person and equipment to do it. You hire a fast, sensitive editor, and you use a desktop DV editing system. The end result, on digital tape, will only need an expensive facility to tidy it up.

That brings the total preliminary budget to roughly £65,000, including all the other bits and pieces, like feeding and insurance. And everyone is paid properly. No deferments; no profit share given away to crew.

The £50,000 movie is a bit of a cheat, because it assumes one person (you) writing, directing, and producing, but if you can do all that yourself (and do it well – cutting corners never saves in the long run) then all you need is £50,000 . . . Go for it.

Baked beans – a series

In most cases, costing a series is much the same as costing a single programme. In the case of a closed series with a fairly short production period, there's not much need to do anything differently. However, a continuing series – or any series with a long production period – should be looked at slightly differently.

Baked beans and television programmes are the same in some respects. To produce the first single can of baked beans could well cost millions: you have to build the factory, employ the workforce, buy the raw materials for the can, design and print the label, buy and cook the beans – and that's before you try to sell any. Of course, as soon as you start selling beans in tens of thousands of cans, you can spread the cost of the plant, machinery, and workforce across the whole output. If your factory cost £1 million to set up and you produce 1 can of beans, then it's a £1 million can of beans (plus the beans themselves). If you produce 10 million cans of beans, then the factory's costs come down to 10p per can. You can do this with television series, too.

There's a basic minimum cost in setting up any programme or film, in terms of research, set building, props buying, pre-production time. In the case of a series, much of this work only has to be done once, and its cost can be spread over the total run of the production.

Series budgets

Assuming the project is financed and ready to go, there will be costs which remain the same whether you produce one episode or one hundred: the basic sets; rigging and lighting the sets; the development costs; casting; music for the signature tune; generic title sequences; executive producers' fees; the writing of the first few scripts; an allowance for scripts commissioned and not used. This isn't an exhaustive list, but it makes the point. Take all these costs and bundle them into a separate budget, the amortisation budget. Once set, this doesn't change, because it's money that is spent or at least committed whatever the run of the show.

Each show will also have its own budget: studio days; production crew; cast; script – everything you'd normally put in – except for the basic set, which is already paid for, and all the pre-production and set-up costs. You put in only the items which have to be paid if there's a show. Everything else is already paid for. What you do put in, however, is a proportion of the set-up costs. If there are 12 shows, each one also has a twelfth of the amort costs assigned to it; if there are 100 shows, each one bears one hundredth of the set-up costs.

Running a car costs a certain amount every year whether or not it ever leaves the garage. You have to tax it, insure it, probably give it at least one service a year to stop it falling apart – not counting its loss of value. But you only pay for fuel, oil, and extra servicing if you drive it. If you drive one mile a year, it may cost you around £500 a mile to run your car. If you drive 10,000 miles, it comes down to about 30p a mile.

The same savings of scale can happen in well-planned, well-run television series. In fact, it's often the only way to get the cost per hour down to what broadcasters expect to pay. It's hard to produce an hour's television for £4000. It's not easy, but considerably easier to produce five hours' television for £20,000.

There's a danger in factory production, too, which underlines the importance of making sure you stay in control and you know what's going on. It's a banal danger, but real, none the less: a series of 50 episodes produced for £8000 per episode, has a total budget of £400,000. That's a lot of money. But £8000 per episode is not a lot of money. It's a great temptation in any production, particularly early on, to be seduced by the availability of large amounts of money. It's important to remember that you have to pay for a lot of things out of it. Don't be like the kids who spend all their monthly pocket money on the first weekend . . .

Summary

Doing a budget is just a long shopping list.

It's tempting to take the budget for a previous similar programme, and just edit it for the new one. However, if you really want to get the budget down, it's better to start from nothing and go through the form putting in only what you need.

The true cost of a programme includes everything:

❏ development
❏ extra producers
❏ production
❏ post-production
❏ costs of finance
❏ insurance

The little things add up to more than you think.

Set-up costs of a series can be spread across the whole series. The more programmes you make, the lower the unit cost of each one.

CHAPTER 4

FINANCE AND DEAL STRUCTURES

There comes a stage when a project becomes real – becomes a 'thing', with a kind of life of its own. Now all you have to do is find the money to pay for it. And of course, you need to know how much money you're going to need. No deal is going to be done without at least a preliminary budget to discuss.

You may have sold the idea to a conventional mass-audience channel with sensible amounts of money to spend on traditional production methods. In that case you won't need to read any further. And there won't be much flexibility over the deal. In this case, as in the good old days when every programme was fully-paid for, and fully-commissioned, there's really only one deal, take it or leave it. The broadcaster's attitude is that they are paying for the programme, and what seems to them to be a generous profit margin (production fee) on top of the prime costs of production; so they own the copyright and all rights of exploitation in perpetuity throughout the universe.

This is still the case with some broadcasters, but, increasingly, television stations are finding that they don't have the cash available to wield the big stick on the deal. They are having to be more flexible in order to get what they want. And of course you do, too.

Every deal is different. There are various familiar ways in which people tend to approach a funding situation, but what has happened before can only be a guide. Particularly in a world where there are so many variables.

There are only two unbreakable rules as far as I'm concerned. The first commandment is *thou shalt not lose money*. You are not in the business of making home movies. You are not in the business of subsidizing television companies. You are there to make a living. You happen to make a living by making films and television, rather than fixing people's plumbing – but you wouldn't expect your plumber to work for the cost of the raw materials, would you? And neither should you.

This seems an obvious thing to say. The problem is, that the job of the legal department in any company – particularly companies bigger than yours – is to maximize their return while minimizing their input – less elegantly put, to screw you if they can. Basically, they will want to give as small a licence fee as they can (think in tens of pounds, if they can get away with it) and take as many rights for that as they can. Your job is to do the opposite for your company. Your problem is that you are one of many little people, and they are the ones with the money. There will always come a point when they could say, 'This is the deal. If you don't like it, we'll get our programmes somewhere else.'

Unless you have exclusive access to something that they want very much, they are always going to win in the end.

However, it isn't normally that clear-cut. The problems really come when an initially acceptable – if borderline – situation becomes eroded. You can be quite sure that if you go over budget, the broadcaster is not going to be the one that pays. Overspends will come out of your pocket – first of all out of your profit, then your fee, then your savings. So don't do deals for honour, or prestige, or because you want to do someone a favour. And don't overspend.

The second commandment is one for survival. *A good deal is one that everyone wants to do again.* If you are big and rich and powerful, perhaps you can afford to go around upsetting people, creating groups of people who never want to see you again. Or maybe you can afford to take big losses in the short term in order to get what you want in the long term. But it's unlikely you'd be reading this, if that were the case. So *try to make relationships, not deals.*

How to approach a funding situation? Clearly the way you make the programme will be influenced by the amount of money available to the budget. Conversely, the amount of money you need will be affected by what you have to do. The relationship between budget and production methods is complex and changes constantly.

Net profit

Before we look at various possible deal structures, a word on net profit. The 'gross' is the total amount of money paid by the buyer for a sale or sales. The 'net' is what's left after deductions. Your share will almost always come from the net.

Definitions of net can vary, both in outline and in detail. In general, before any net is paid from a sale or sales, distribution costs and fees, programme production costs, and costs of finance, including any deferred fees are all subtracted. There's a fuller definition from a contract in the appendices.

However you work, a clear understanding of what people mean by 'net profit' is crucial. Whether you accept a full commission, or whether you are completely on your own, how you define net profit can make an enormous difference to your bank balance. So can your position in the order in which things are removed from the gross, and so can the number of things which are actually accounted against the gross on the way. One reason (of the many reasons) that artistes' and directors' fees in feature films have risen so massively, is that most people have learnt (often the hard way) that a percentage of the net profits sounds very enticing, but that there might never be any net profits.

Distributors, production companies, accountants can make quite sure that nothing ever trickles through to the 'back end' if they are so minded. So the usual solution is to take the money now. Hence the massive fees. Better to have 10 per cent of something now, than 100 per cent of something which may or may not be more, and may or may not ever appear at some time in the future. The mortgage lenders and the butcher, the baker and the candlestick maker are not going to wait until your share of net profits comes through.

I Fully commissioned programmes

The most straightforward way of financing a programme or series is to get a broadcaster to pay for it all. One-stop shopping means that, with luck, the development period is short; the deal is simple; and everything is done quite rapidly.

Beware of the musical chairs syndrome, in which you get an enthusiastic response from a commissioning editor, and engage in protracted discussions about exactly how and when your series is going to be funded, only to find that your contact leaves the company, causing the sudden death of your project.

A major problem, of course, can be that you find that the broadcaster can't afford your programme in the first place. This is a particular worry with some of the newer channels; but you can also find this on certain programme strands in even the biggest broadcasters. Some of their internal costing structures are byzantine, to say the least, and working with them can make you feel a little like Alice in Wonderland.

So be sure to get down to talking numbers as early as possible in the conversation. And don't be put off with general statements like, 'Well, you know that our budgets are very low.' or worse, 'This is very important to us. This is going to be a flagship series for our new season.'

'Low budget' can mean £75,000 per half hour. Or it can mean £1,000 per half hour. It all depends on where you're starting from.

Equally, although the fact that your programme is going to lead a schedule can be flattering, it also means that the commissioning process is likely to be very demanding. However much money they put in, they're going to want a lot for it. And if their idea of a big budget is £12,000 per hour, there may well be tears before bedtime.

Don't be put off. Most of the time everything works out very well. However, there are pitfalls to be wary of – and it's very easy to be blinded by the enthusiasm of actually getting a programme going, and just to say 'yes' to everything.

A full commission is one of the two simplest ways of financing a project (the other one is paying for it all yourself. More of that later). The implications are similarly simple. If the broadcaster funds the series, it may be simpler to get financed in the first place, but doesn't belong to you. You make it for an agreed price, out of which sum the production is paid for (including any fees payable to you or your colleagues as a budget line, such as director, editor, researcher); and your company gets a production fee which is an agreed (or more usually, imposed) percentage of the production budget. If you go over budget, you may or may not be able to recover the cost from the broadcaster. If you come in under budget, you'll normally expect to split the saving 50/50 with the broadcaster.

The broadcaster owns the programme completely. It can be shown forever as many times as they like. Normally they will insist that the copyright is theirs, and all ancillary rights, too – including spin-offs like merchandising and books. If they sell it to other broadcasters in other countries, you can expect to get a percentage of the net profit, probably around 30 per cent.

Discussing fully-commissioned programmes as an option makes it sound as if any producer at any time stands at a crossroads where she or he can choose to take an offer from a broadcaster, or to finance the project in some other way. In reality, of course, this is far from the case, and one of the main reasons for examining other ways of financing projects is in order to get something happening at all. In the end there are probably around half a dozen commissioning editors in the UK to approach with any given programme – whether children's, primetime drama, documentary. They are all (a) inundated with suggestions – most of them rubbish, it's true, but still many times more than they can use, and (b) they don't have that much screen time to fill. Children's ITV produces three new drama series a year. They receive more than 2000 proposals for these three slots. We live in a country with too little air-time and too many producers. We need to find ways around this log-jam.

Copyright

Copyright is a difficult, but important question; and it's increasingly important in the multi-channel world, where deal structures can become quite complicated. The big traditional broadcasters, like the BBC, will require you to assign all the copyright in the programme they commission over to them. If you protest, they will say that in the real world it isn't the ownership of the copyright that matters, but the share of the exploitation. You get the same percentage of profit, it doesn't matter whose name is on the copyright line.

Well that's true, up to a point. But if it were as absolutely true as they want you to believe, why are they so bothered about controlling all the copyright? It's partly about control. If you renege on a deal, and they own the copyright, then they still have the programme – or the rights to the underlying property. Equally, once the copyright is assigned to them, they can renege on the deal, and you are in a very difficult position – because you don't own your project any more. Of course, you could take them to court – but how much time and money is that going to cost?

Contracts are funny things. They are there to set everything out so that all parties to a deal know what they're agreeing to and what its implications are. They attempt to consider every possible future problem and provide an answer now, to save trouble later. But when it does all go wrong – or one of your partners breaks the contract – what are you going to do about it? Can you afford the time and money to pursue the contract through the courts? A contract is ultimately only worth the amount of money you're prepared to throw at it if it all goes horribly wrong.

The more important point about copyright for independent producers and production companies is that it counts as an asset. The world of film and television production companies is very strange to people who work in financial institutions. They can understand a factory buying machinery to produce baked beans. There you have a clear investment in plant and machinery, which can be sold if the company gets into difficulties; and you have a clear product: so many thousands of cans of beans a day. As long as the beans are produced on time and sell, then everyone is happy – particularly if you sell more beans this year than you did last.

Film and television trades in ideas. You can't put an idea in a can and sell it. That's not true, because we put ideas into cans all the time. However, the can itself is worth nothing. It's the idea inside it that has value, because that's what's being traded. Maybe it's not so different from beans, after all.

A very large and successful independent producer decided it needed to raise some finance on the stock market and put up a portion of the company for sale. There was enormous initial interest from financial institutions, because it was a very high-profile company with a continuous stream of popular production. But suddenly the interest dried up – because the financiers realized that the company wasn't worth anything. Yes, they produced hundreds of hours of television a year – but they owned none of the copyright. Their only income was from production fees. Their entire prosperity depended on the continuing health and popularity of the two talented writers who were at the heart of the company. The past didn't belong to them. Yes, there was the profit share from the broadcaster, but basically, they had no reliable source of income from their previous work. They had no catalogue.

That company changed its strategy, and insists on keeping as much of the copyright in its productions as it can. Copyright is a balance sheet item by which a production company is valued; because copyright can be bought and sold, and the income from programmes in which you own the copyright come, at least theoretically, to you. So don't give it away without a struggle.

2 Paying for it yourself

An even simpler way of getting a project off the ground is to pay for everything yourself. If you fund it all on your own, then it all belongs to you, and you get 100 per cent of the profits. You also run 100 per cent of the risk of making a 100 per cent loss, and of ending up with an expensive home-movie on your hands.

If you have the money, it's entirely up to you. If I were advising you, I'd suggest that you attempt to make at least one major pre-sale to a distributor or broadcaster before you spend your money. That way you know that someone wants it. And where one goes, others will follow. The first question is often, 'Who else has shown it?' There's a tremendous reluctance amongst buyers to be the first. Television is increasingly full of people (often in suits) who spend enormous amounts of time and effort in avoiding making brave decisions.

'No budget'

Certainly, it's possible to make a movie (documentary or drama) for nothing, or next to nothing. You beg a lot of favours from people, and buy the lunches out of your own pocket.

If you're organized, and have a good project, using some of the techniques discussed here; and if you give people a good time, then you can end up with something that everyone is pleased with.

However, it's a way of getting something going; but it isn't a way of making a living. You can do it once or twice, but everyone needs to pay the rent, too, and nobody can afford to give too much away, however much they might like helping people try to achieve something. In the end, things have to be paid for.

This kind of programme making is a way of starting out. You have a calling card, and you might even make money on selling the programme you've made for nothing – after all, any sale is going to be profit, isn't it? Sometimes it really does work – the people with serious money beat a path to your door waving cheque-books and you're off on a career of big-budget movies. But you can't rely on that happening; and you can't live off favours. So, you've done it once. What do you do next, while you're waiting for Hollywood to call?

The core idea of this book is to suggest techniques for getting projects produced where everyone is properly paid, has a good time, and nobody owes anyone any favours.

3 The third way

Between the two extremes of getting a single broadcaster to pay for the whole thing, and paying for it all yourself, there are almost as many possibilities as there are projects.

What would the ideal situation be? One in which you were in full control of the production process; where you are sure that the result would be seen; that it earns more money than it cost to make; and that you are the person or company who receives all that money.

Committees are death. The key to being in control of the production process is to involve as few decision-making people as possible. Every additional financing partner will want (and deserve) a say in the way the programme is made. This doesn't just affect the politics of the production, and how pleasant or unpleasant the experience is; committees can have a dramatic effect on the cost of the production. Very simply put, if there are lengthy discussions on set, or in the cutting room, no work is being done, and expensive people and equipment are sitting and standing around idle. The schedule goes first, and the budget follows as night follows day. Really efficient production must be very tightly controlled, with all the important decisions being made before the money is spent.

Because changing your mind is expensive, too. Everyone makes mistakes. Things always turn out differently from the way they were planned; but being flexible and realistic is not the same as allowing a habit of expensive alterations to develop. Certain sections of our industry habitually work in this way – a set is built. 'No, it's not what we wanted.' and rebuilt. A scene is shot, and re-shot. Film production by trial and error. It's a production method which can, in the end, still produce world-beating results. But it's expensive and inefficient. We can't afford it.

So, in order to come as close to the ideal programme and money-making situation as possible, the number of producers needs to be restricted.

Distributor-led programming

Case history: *Gumdrop*

Our animation series of 26 × 5 minutes based on the *Gumdrop* books by Val Biro worked out very well.

First of all the production budget was low. The production process was kept deliberately very simple. We had approached a number of broadcasters and home-video distributors in the UK. The responses had generally been positive, but we still had no commitment. The broadcasters said they had no spare money for a while; the home video distributors said they needed a television showing, then they'd take it. The question was, how long were we prepared to wait?

I had also been discussing the project with Ravensburger Film + TV, a German producer and distributor, whom I'd met at MIP-TV previously. Ravensburger were happy to co-produce the series with us. The arrangement we came to was:

- ❏ Ravensburger contributed 50 per cent of the budget. This was partly an advance on distribution fees, and partly an investment in exchange for a profit share.
- ❏ They would be able to sell the series in Germany wherever and however they liked. Proceeds of these sales did not go into the profit share, they would kept by Ravensburger.
- ❏ Similarly we could do what we liked in the UK without involving Ravensburger.
- ❏ Ravensburger would distribute the series in the rest of the world, and revenue would be split 52/48 per cent in our favour.

Normally a distributor would expect to take a distribution fee of between 25 per cent and 35 per cent of the total value of any sale they make (the gross), and to recoup the costs of making the sale, which, if it's not capped, could approach another 10 per cent. A pessimistic view of the costs of distribution could give the distributor 45 per cent of the gross in any case, so a total of 48 per cent as a combined distribution fee and profit share is a good deal. Well, we were all happy with it, which is the important point. It is a deal we would all do again.

Where was the other half of the money coming from? The short answer is that we didn't have it. However, in this case we went against our own advice, and deferred our own costs, since we were fairly confident of making a quick sale once the series existed as boxes of tape rather than pieces of paper. Most of the cash costs were accounted for by Ravensburger's contribution, so the only people we owed money to at the end of the (fairly short) production period were ourselves.

Once they saw the series, Channel 4 agreed to take it. We sold them a licence for four years, and that paid our deferred costs. So any further sales we made were going to be profit.

Now that there was a television showing, the home video distributors were interested, and we insisted on a distribution advance from them. It's always a good idea to insist on some kind of advance from a distributor, even if you don't need it to produce the programme. First of all, it means that you have at least some money now. Distributors, like publishers, usually pay you every six months. By the time the packing is designed, the cassettes have been duplicated and sold into the shops, the first payment is likely to be nearly a year after you sign the contract. If you negotiate an advance, you would expect to get that on signing.

Secondly, if a distributor has paid you a (non-returnable) advance against the sales they expect to make, it's in their interest to work harder so that they recoup the money they've laid out.

In the case of *Gumdrop* the home video distribution advance was 100 per cent profit for us.

Subsequently we sold Gaelic language rights, satellite television rights, and also received our share of revenue from the sales that Ravensburger made. The amounts of money involved were not huge, but there's no doubt that the whole process was a happy one.

There's no reason why the same format shouldn't work with any production. Particularly if your end really does have either its own source of cash, or a broadcaster who will put up money in advance.

Production politics

As soon as you're not asking a broadcaster to pay for the entire production cost, as in the fully-commissioned model, you are in a position of much greater negotiating strength. If your broadcaster is only putting in half the money, or a third of the money, they can only reasonably expect to have a half or third voice in the way the programme is produced.

However, there's still a very finely-graded scale of influence to be judged and handled. If the broadcaster is simply pre-buying a series, and you're dealing with the acquisitions department, then possibly you'll be left completely alone to get on with things. However, this way you'll be getting the least amount of money from the deal.

At the other extreme, consider the situation where a broadcaster of your acquaintance has a project for which they are looking for extra finance, which you provide or arrange. It can work very well. The broadcaster should be – and sometimes is – grateful that you are making something possible that they can't otherwise afford. It can also happen that the broadcaster feels resentful that they are unable to provide all the finance for their own programme, and they behave as if they were fully commissioning it. The politics of situations like these can become complex.

The *Gumdrop* model of financing is becoming more and more common as the balance of power we were talking about before continues to shift.

Distributors are increasingly expecting to provide some form of finance as part of a pre-production deal. If you already have two thirds or more of the money in place from pre-sales or other forms of finance, then a distributor will often be happy to provide 'top-up' finance for the remaining portion. This will be a distribution advance, which they will recoup in first position. That means no-one else involved in the project gets any money from sales until the distributor has their money back from your share of the revenue. That is, they take their normal distribution fees first, and then recoup the advance from the amounts that would have been passed on to you.

Some distributors will buy rights to certain territories outright. This tends to occur quite often for complicated, low-value regions, where a local distributor can get most out of the area: the Middle East, and Latin America are two examples.

A number of larger production companies are also distributors, and will go ahead and just produce a series having made only minor pre-sales. They will continue to pre-sell during the production process, and, if they are lucky, might have covered the cost of production by the time the programmes are ready for delivery.

Case history: Sponsorship

The principal source of finance for our documentary travel series, *Cafés of Europe*, was sponsorship. Sponsorship can be an interesting way of financing television, but it can also be politically very complex.

In the UK there is a tremendous nervousness about advertiser-funded programming. The rules about what may or may not be shown and done are strict. If you approach a broadcaster with a project which has the involvement of a sponsor, the broadcaster is likely to say, 'Thanks very much for the sponsor, we'll take over here.'

Sponsorship of programmes in the UK is very rarely truly sponsorship of the programme, but of the programme slot. The purpose of the many rules circumscribing what sponsors are allowed to do is to make sure that the sponsor has no editorial influence on the programme, and can't use it as a cheap way of advertising their product.

What? If it isn't a way of advertising their product, why should a sponsor be interested in the programme? The answer to that is that sponsorship of television is comparatively under-developed in the UK for exactly that reason. What does happen is so-called 'lifestyle' sponsorship. Sponsors are allowed and encouraged to support programmes that appeal to the same kind of target group as their product. A series aimed at young people with lots of disposable income will be attractive to the fashion industry even though clothes are never mentioned, because the brand's name is continually exposed to the target market for the brand, too.

In other countries almost anything can be sponsored. Advertisers are allowed to make programmes – and indeed give them away, in a barter process, where a channel might give an advertising agency, or even a manufacturer a time-slot to fill – perhaps two hours each Friday evening – and the advertising agency provides the programmes at no cost to the channel, as long as they also keep the revenue from the advertising during the slot. There are advantages and disadvantages to this approach, and the practice tends to ebb and flow around the world.

In the real world, sponsors want television exposure. Television channels need programming. If a series is produced; if it's good, and something the channel want, and they simply buy a licence, as long as the sponsorship is not intrusive and doesn't actually break any rules, the channel is unlikely to object.

That was the way we made our *Cafés* series. It was pre-sold to a satellite channel in the UK, which unlocked the sponsorship money. This wasn't quite enough to make the series, even with our skills at making something brilliant out of almost nothing. Some of the series would have been filmed in Vienna, in any case, so we involved a local television station in Vienna as a co-producer. They provided a crew for three days, and on-line edit facilities – but no cash – in exchange for which we gave them all rights to the whole series within Austria. That was enough to make the difference we needed, and we went ahead. We remained in full control of the production itself – and also owned all rights in the programme outside Austria, since the sponsors are interested in exposure, not in rights ownership.

Co-production

Co-production tends to have a slightly different meaning, depending on where you're starting from. If a broadcaster like the BBC enters into a co-production deal, they are typically using it as a way of raising extra production finance for a programme or series that they are likely to be producing in any case. In commercial terms, it gives the project a head-start in the international market, and the co-production deal almost certainly raises more money from the co-producing territory than a straightforward sale would do. In this event, the co-producing partner is also most likely to be another broadcaster.

Co-production for independent producers has a more co-operative atmosphere about it. As always, there are many different ways in which deals can be structured, but the best arrangements tend to be simple ones where it is quite clear what all partners are getting out of the deal.

You have a project which you are trying to finance. You know how much money you need. The project has some interest for audiences in, let's say Canada, where you happen to know a production company, so you suggest doing it as a co-production with them.

It's clear what you are going to get out of the arrangement – money from Canada to make your programme. But what is your Canadian partner getting out of the deal? It's worth looking at things the other way round occasionally. If a Canadian producer had come to you looking for a co-producer for a project, what would you want? Probably more than just the pleasure of handing over your cash (or raising money on their behalf).

You'd probably want some production input, because you are a producer, not a banker. You'd certainly want to have enough creative input to be sure that the result would be suitable for audiences in your country.

We have financed a children's drama series as an Anglo-Canadian co-production. The basic deal is similar to the *Gumdrop* deal, but different. Basically we split everything down the middle with our partner in Canada. We each found half the finance; we each keep our own territory to do with what we can; and all profits from all sources go into a single pot which we then split 50/50.

Filming takes place in the UK, and post-production in Canada. A number of cast and key personnel are Canadian, which has all sorts of advantages for the Canadian end of the financing, because it qualifies as a treaty co-production.

Treaty co-production

Various combinations of countries have signed co-production treaties with each other. The major benefit of a production that qualifies as a treaty co-production is that it is counted as a national production in both countries. That means that it qualifies for the same tax benefits and subsidies as a production that is entirely produced in the respective country. In the case of Canada that is quite significant, because it gives access to the funds of Telefilm Canada, and various other local film and television production funds. In the case of the UK it means very little – except that your partner is able to take advantage of their local benefits, of course.

However, the application procedure can be tiresome. A fairly large number of forms need to be completed, and conditions have to be met. If the nature of the production changes, and these conditions are no longer met, then the programme's status as a national production can be removed. There are variations amongst the treaties, and copies of them can be had from the Department of Trade and Industry (DTI). Normally the most important clauses concern the minimum financial input from the minority partner – normally something like 30 per cent; and require a credible level of creative input from the minority partner, too.

The European Union

Although the tax and subsidy situation for producers in the UK swings from time to time between the cool and the luke-warm, as a member of the European Union, British producers do have two benefits.

The European Union actually puts quite a lot of money into subsidizing what is technically called the 'audio-visual' industries – including film, television, multimedia. It's a politically-led attempt to support and develop a powerful enough industry to counter the effects of American cultural imperialism. Or, put at a more day-to-day level, to encourage an industry that is healthy enough to produce a quantity and type of programming that can compete with the American exports that it's just so easy for broadcasters to buy when they are desperate to fill their schedules with anything watchable.

As citizens of a member state of the European Union, British producers, too, have access to these funds. The precise conditions under which these funds give out grants are constantly changing, of course, but usually they're in the form of interest-free loans, some of which only have to be repaid if the project makes money.

However, since these funds are controlled by a multi-national bureaucracy, applicants have to jump through many hoops and complete a great many forms before they get the money. It's easier after the first time, but some people may feel that it isn't worth it. Put the same effort into making a direct sale to a broadcaster or distributor, and you may have enough to make the programme anyway.

One other benefit to British producers of being members of the European Union is that, under the European law that allows for free movement of goods and services throughout the member states, a co-production treaty with any one member state may include another co-production partner from within the European Union without losing national status. If I involve a German co-producer in my Anglo-Canadian treaty co-production, the production still qualifies as British, just as it would without the German partner.

Hidden sales

Selling or co-producing complete programmes is not the only way to finance a series. Light entertainment shows are very often made in different versions in different countries, with the programme's originator receiving a format fee for the use of the original format and idea. This can be something of a minefield. Some production companies, notably the UK-based Action Time, have made a considerable success of licensing format rights to game shows that they developed and originally produced in the UK. However, there are also cases of people who feel that a format belongs to them, that a series produced in another country was making use of their format, but they were still unable to persuade the courts that they were owed any money by the producer of the new series.

The underlying debate is, of course, about copyright. There is no copyright in an idea. The copyright lies in the work which is produced as the result of an idea. It can be argued that not enough lies in the format of a television show to make it a unique piece of work. It depends on which side of the argument you're on.

Fraggle Rock

There is a kind of mid-ground which is a much safer place to stand. *Fraggle Rock* was a children's series from Jim Henson Productions involving a lighthouse keeper, a number of muppets, and various film/video inserts. The series originated in the United States but was sold around the world.

What was interesting was that what was sold was the format, and tape of the inserts and story scenes. The series was then remade in a studio in each of the countries it was sold to, incorporating these elements, and with a local actor playing the 'anchor' character.

Play School

The BBC's pre-school series *Play School* was sold in a similar way. Buyers bought the scripts, the format, and the film/video inserts, and produced their own version of the programmes.

Finding partners

This book is about making things happen. You can get programmes made by being able to produce them very cheaply, or
by involving others in a co-production, or a combination of
both.

Warehousing

Another option open to small companies without much of a
track record of their own, is to develop a relationship with a
larger company in their own country. This kind of arrangement,
often known as 'warehousing' can often be a good way of getting
started, but tends not to be very satisfactory in the long run,
because the big company is always going to get the most out of it.
Relationships with other companies with the same interests in
the same country are always problematic, because, however
much you might try to make it seem otherwise, you are always
going to be in direct competition with each other. The same kind
of relationship with another company in a different country has
a much better chance of being useful in the long term, because
the two companies complement each other, and provide two
markets for the same project, rather than a competition for the
same market.

But there aren't any simple answers. Generally speaking, it's
worth trying almost anything once – but be careful without being
greedy. And be realistic. In the end it's better to have 10 per cent
of something, than 100 per cent of nothing.

So how do you go about finding co-production partners in other
countries? It will be time-consuming; but take the attitude that
you are building relationships. If nothing comes of the contact
now, it's still one other person you can just call some time in the
future with a different project. Nothing is ever wasted. At the
very least you gain a deeper perspective on the industry
worldwide.

The Internet

Start with the Internet. Production companies who have some kind of a Web presence are likely to be more open-minded than average. It's also astonishing how much film and television finance and support information there is to be found very easily – even if the bias is very much North American.

Markets and trade fairs

MIP

Go at least once to MIP-TV or MIPCOM. It's expensive, but it's worth it, as long as you plan it properly beforehand. MIP-TV in April and MIPCOM in October each year are arguably the most important international programme markets of the year, and are increasingly populated by independent producers.

The markets are so busy now that it's a waste of time going unless you already have at least enough meetings firmly booked before you go to make your visit worthwhile. The average length of a meeting at MIP is about ten minutes, and anyone really worth talking to (programme buyers in particular) will have every ten-minute slot of the week filled before they arrive. So the chances of just walking up to the Big Cheese and selling your idea, or completed series, are practically nil.

Having said that, you *always* meet people you would meet no other way, and these unexpected encounters are often the real benefit of going. The *MIP-TV Guide* is probably the best directory of international television there is, and comes free with the (roughly £1000 per company) registration.

And you get a view of the world's television that you can't get by sitting in an office at home. MIP-TV always ends in a feeling of euphoria because you've spent a week with people who are actually making programmes – actually *doing* things. The trick is to follow it all up and turn that euphoria into programmes.

Using the press

It goes without saying that you need to read the trade papers and acquire at least one general international production directory.

But there's no easy way. Armed with all of this information, it still all comes down to making cold calls, meeting people, talking projects.

I've spent a long time on acquiring and managing finances, because that's what it's like out there. Making the programme is easy; it's selling the idea and raising the money to do it that takes the time. But don't give up. It's the same for everyone.

Revenue – the bottom line

What kind of income are we likely to get worldwide from sales of our series? The advantage of working in television rather than theatrical movies, is that it is possible to make a reasonably accurate minimum revenue projection. Television stations pay known amounts for programming, and an intelligent projection of where a series is likely to sell can result in a fairly accurate idea of what you're going to get over five or ten years.

The disadvantage is that sales are unlikely to reach the heights that popular movies bring in at the box office. With a few exceptions, large amounts of money are made in television by selling large amounts of programming, not by getting outrageously high prices for any one programme.

At current prices, a two-hour TV movie could reasonably expect to take about $1.8 million over ten years. Half of that revenue is likely to come from sales made in the first three years. From that the distributor's 30–35 per cent needs to be deducted, which leaves around $1.2 million.

In the same way, a four-hour mini-series might bring in $3 million to the producer; and a 26-part series of one-hour episodes, around $400,000 per episode.

For animation, a series of 13 × half-hours should achieve at least $150,000 per half hour.

'Lifestyle' programming is often more problematic, because it tends to be of more local interest (with the possible exception of travel programmes) and to go into low-value slots: revenue of around $75,000 per half hour for a series might be reasonable.

The earnings of a single documentary are less easy to predict, since single programmes are hard to sell. You could probably expect around $300,000 for a one-hour programme.

These are all deliberately conservative numbers – you would hope to do better, but shouldn't expect to. Clearly you can't expect early retirement on this basis, but it *is* possible to make programmes and make a profit from sales alone if you're able to control the budget well enough.

The way to make more out of sales revenue is to involve a broadcaster as a co-production partner. If the broadcaster contributes 50 per cent of an £800,000 TV movie budget in exchange for a licence and 25 per cent of the net profit, you are left with £400,000 to recover and 75 per cent of the profit. If the movie makes £800,000 worldwide, then your share is £300,000 after the cost of production has been recouped.

If you had made the movie all on your own, then the £800,000 worldwide revenue would cover the production costs, but there would be no profit. You would, however, have received your producer's fees from within the movie's budget, so it isn't as if you were making the film for nothing.

The deal – a summary

A reminder of the basic options:

- ❏ **Fully commissioned:** the broadcaster pays for it all. You own nothing but get a minority share of the net profit, if there is any.
- ❏ **Fully self-funded:** you pay for it all and own it all absolutely. You also take all the risk of not making enough in sales to cover the budget.
- ❏ **Partly self-funded:** you find your own finance for a portion of the budget, or you defer certain costs, and fund the rest with an advance from a distributor, or a broadcast pre-sale, or both. A distributor might buy rights for certain territories outright.
- ❏ **Co-production:** in its simplest form, you enter into an agreement with a producer in another country, who find half the money from their territory, and you provide the other half from a broadcaster in your own. In practice, there may well be more than two partners involved.

If you make the programmes very cost-efficiently, you may find that three pre-sales could cover the production cost. Any further sales are then all profit.

Most programmes should continue to sell for a number of years – normally five to ten years after completion, sometimes longer (particularly with animation). The ideal situation might be to try to make sure to cover your costs in the first wave of sales – the first two to three years – and gradually build up a catalogue of programmes where the remaining sales provide a revenue stream of pure profits . . .

RESEARCH AND SCRIPT

At last the project is financed. There's a fixed amount of cash available. And there's a delivery date. The problem now is to produce the promised series and still make a profit to invest in the time it will take to develop the next series.

Research

Whether or not the budget allows for a person actually described as 'researcher', every production requires research: factual research, to do with the programme's content; and production research, by which I mean research work necessary in setting up the production ready for filming. Here, as everywhere, there are no magic wands. The way to stay within the budget is to remain focused; to think before you spend; and to be efficient – don't waste time rushing off in all directions on the chance that it will be worthwhile.

In the basic subject research for a factual programme it can be very easy to be seduced by interesting side issues, and to spend a great deal of time following threads which either lead to a dead end, or (worse) lead in a different direction altogether from the one you need to take.

The whole point about research is that you don't know what the answers are before you start researching. Naturally any process of research will (or should) uncover the unexpected, and may even contradict the original assumption from which you started out. If that happens, it would be completely wrong to attempt to force the new information to prove an argument you now know to be false. You have to be true to your sources, and to the story as you see it.

However, it's also important to remember the purpose of the research. Interesting though a new discovery might be, if it isn't relevant to the programme you're making, then you should leave it alone.

From the very beginning of a production to the very end, you encounter countless suggestions, possibilities, offers, confusions. The producer's job (and the director's) is to mark out the path of clarity through the bright jungle of confusion. But that is not to say that the path is already marked before you begin your journey. Decisions have to be made all the time, and it can be the hardest thing to reject a new and interesting nugget of information – but it has to be done if the new nugget is not relevant to the programme.

There are various ways in which you can save yourself trouble, time, and expense in the factual research for a programme.

The simplest and most cost-effective way is to make a series set in a world, or based on a subject that you know personally very well. If you are the series expert, you have no need to pay others to tell you what you already know.

Nearly as straightforward is to find a single person who can do the same thing for you.

The least sensible thing to do, from the point of view of cost-efficient programming, is to start from complete ignorance and to spend – or pay someone else to spend – a long time re-inventing the wheel.

Having said that, pretending to re-invent the wheel is often a useful way of forcing yourself to take a new perspective on a subject area which seems familiar – forcing yourself to forget what you had to learn and think from the point of view of someone seeing for the first time. In fact, I'd recommend this as a way of keeping your subject fresh, and of avoiding the danger of missing out important elements which you (the expert) might take for granted, but which are not obvious to your audience.

However, in the world of programme-making, our aim is to work as efficiently as we can. It makes much more sense to buy existing expertise in one package, than to pay to acquire it haphazardly over a long period.

Cafés: research for a travel series

This is a particularly straightforward example, since our *Cafés of Europe* series was, in some ways, the film of the book. A colleague with whom we'd often worked before is a restaurateur and writer of restaurant guide books. He was in the process of putting together a book guide to the cafés of Europe, so much of the factual research had already been done.

We chose three cities to cover in the television series – Paris, Madrid, and Vienna – which meant that we had two programmes on each city. Which cafés should be featured was decided in consultation with the person who had been responsible for the book research for the city. This person was then asked to visit each of the places we'd chosen (we made sure that we selected more than we thought we would need) and persuade them that they really did want to let us in to film at their busiest time.

Asylum: research for a documentary

In a documentary on the plight of asylum-seekers in Germany, and the system that deals with them, in a sense the research *was* the film. Our background research was performed with a combination of print and Internet searching, followed up with telephone conversation with people both in the UK and in Germany. We then set up a recce trip to meet some of the people we proposed filming, and to confirm that the provisional shape we'd put on the programme was going to make sense.

This shape was designed as a flexible running order. That is, while we knew enough now to know what we expected to find, the narrative structure could still cope with reality if a different emphasis should emerge during filming. We were not intending to force what we eventually found in the filming to match pre-conceived ideas.

The recce was short – which means it was inexpensive. By the end of it we knew enough of our targeted people and places to be able to fine-tune the rest of the setting up of the filming on the telephone.

During the quite intensive filming process we listened to people. The range of interviewees was quite wide, and we responded to what people told us, both in terms of being able to adjust the questions we asked in later interviews, and in terms of the purely visual material we shot. The result was a film that was truly documentary, in that very little was actually finalized before the filming – but within a controlled framework, so that this could be achieved efficiently in terms of schedule, and therefore, budget.

This production process was *not* the same as 'making it up as you go along'. While we didn't know exactly what was going to be said by all our interviewees – and would certainly not have sought to influence them – our research meant that we did have a good idea of what we expected, and consequently a flexible but well-developed narrative structure. We'll look later at the editing process for this kind of production.

The way to be efficient in researching productions – and therefore manage to produce good quality on a low budget, is to choose subjects where you can gain a thorough and balanced view of a subject without lengthy or geographically widespread research. In no way is this to advocate skimping research in order to make it easier or cheaper on the programme. The strategy is to acquire the necessary knowledge in easily accessible places. And it certainly doesn't mean that everything should be accepted without question. Once again – there's no substitute for proper thought and preparation. Thinking things out saves money. Big budget attitudes tend to use money as a substitute for thought.

Internet searches

This is a book about television, not about the Internet, but I consider the Internet to be such an important resource to every programme-maker, at any budget level, that it's worth spending some time on considering it.

First, and most basic, you can save an enormous amount in postage expenses by sending scripts around the countryside – indeed, the world – by e-mail. I have written scripts for productions made in Canada, and there just wouldn't have been time to perform the work with any other means of communication – except perhaps overnight courier delivery, which isn't exactly a low-budget way to work.

In the mid 1980s there were various databases available for on-line searching. 'Profile' was one of them. It contained the full text of a number of newspapers, and it was an incredibly useful tool. In fifteen minutes of searching, you could find information on your chosen subject that you had no idea existed. And because it was an organized, electronic database, you would have no chance of finding it any other way – certainly it would have taken days of looking through the original newspapers, even if they were available. The only drawback was that these searches cost around £3 per minute. It was worth every penny, but it did make you very focused about what you were looking for.

Many people complain that they're constantly doing Internet searches, and they never find what they want. All they come up with is rubbish. Well, I'm constantly doing Internet searches, and I've never been entirely unsuccessful. Of course there's a lot of rubbish. But the Internet is not tidily indexed and catalogued. It's more like a nature reserve than a garden, but the stuff is (mostly) there somewhere. At least you should be able to find leads to the information or the contacts you want.

Search strategies

There are dozens of search engines, all attempting a more or less complete view of the World Wide Web. But the Web is so vast, and growing so quickly, that much of it is unlikely ever to be indexed at all by the search engines.

However, let's go with what we have. Search engines are divided into two fundamentally different groups. One sort, like Compaq's Altavista, or Google, send out electronic robots across the Web, reading all the pages they find (to a greater or lesser extent) and compiling a vast index of all the words they find, so that if you look for the word 'television' you'll be presented with a list of every occurrence of the word in all the documents on the web that the robots have found.

The other kind of search engine, like Yahoo, is compiled by humans, and arranges web sites it finds, or is requested to catalogue, into subject headings, much more like a real library.

Both have their advantages and disadvantages. If you look for 'television' on Yahoo, you'd get a selection which seemed much more relevant, because you'd be getting their subject headings. But you might not find the report on television and violence that you were looking for and which Altavista's method would give you.

Either search would give you much too much, and probably be headed by a list of fan-sites you don't want. So how to search effectively . . .

First use a so-called meta search engine. Meta search engines query several search engines at once with your search terms, so that you get the best of both methods of indexing. There are some meta-search engines on the Web itself. There are also several you can run on your machine, which has the advantage that you can save and refine the search off-line.

The Internet changes so quickly that there's always a danger that a statement is out of date as soon as it is made: Copernic (www.copernic.com) is a good meta-search program.

Second, think very carefully about the key words you search for. A single word is rarely going to be any good. A search for 'television' is unlikely to produce a manageable result. On the other hand, too many words are likely to restrict the search so much you get nothing. Three or four key words are probably a good idea: for instance, 'television children animation australia'.

Beware of assuming that everyone means the same thing you do. You're putting together a series to do with geology. A search for 'rock' is likely to produce more music than geology.

Enclose phrases or titles in quotation marks. A search for 'Fraggle Rock' will produce only results with the programme's title in them.

Advanced searches

These are all simple searches. If you think carefully about your key words, simple searches will probably produce fairly effective results most of the time. However, many search engines will let you conduct advanced searches, using Boolean queries: AND OR NOT.

In Altavista, for example, you can choose to do an advanced search.

AND

Actually simple searches assume AND in them; that is, looking for documents which include all the key words. Some of them, less usefully in my view, also include OR as a default, so your results will not only include references with all your key words, but also those with only one of them – which is, after all, exactly what you were trying to avoid.

OR

This can be very useful if properly used to control a restricted search: film OR television. Often it's more useful when combined with AND: 'animation AND film OR television'.

NOT

(Often used in conjunction with AND.) Particularly useful when you know that there are alternatives which you don't want to be bothered with. 'Star Wars AND film AND NOT Reagan', for example will do something to confine the star wars research to the movie, and exclude the Strategic Defense Initiative. Or the other way around 'star wars AND NOT film OR movie'.

Brackets

You can also become even more sophisticated by using brackets in the mathematical mode to group concepts: 'Star Wars AND NOT (Skywalker OR Vader)'.

Roots

In most search engines you can treat the word you enter as a root. That is if you enter 'car*' as a search term you will find not only references to do with cars, but also carriages, carrots, caramel, and so on. Some search engines treat any key word as a root, which isn't always helpful. It is most useful when you want to include both singular and plural versions of a word: 'film' and 'films' will both be returned by film*; but 'film' will not be returned by 'films'

Alternatively, you can sometimes specify a single character with '?'. 'Car?' will produce 'car' or 'cars' but not 'carriage'.

These are standard search concepts which work with any proper indexing system. You may already have a program that will index the documents on your own computer, where you can have a go.

There's no substitute for trying things out; and it would be foolish to ignore the Internet as a wonderful source of information. In doing research for the programme on asylum seekers I was able to discover a great deal about the system in various countries; all sorts of statistics; a large number of newspaper articles – and, most important, find out who the people to talk to might be, both on the side of the authorities, and of the pressure groups.

It would be wrong to restrict all your research to the Internet; but it would be equally wrong to miss it out altogether – and certainly more expensive.

The other use of the Internet is to have a presence there for yourself. The independent video-based movie, *The Blair Witch Project*, was famously not only made for next to nothing, but what finance there was is supposed to have come through the popularity of its web site.

The wonderful thing about the Internet is that anyone can just put up a web site, and the whole world can see it. The problem is that the whole world doesn't know it's there.

As we've seen, the web is growing so rapidly that the indexing robots can't keep up with it any more. Enormous sections of the web will probably never be indexed while they're alive.

You can help the visibility of your site by submitting it to as many search engines as you can – either by buying a program to do it for you, or even by paying someone else to do it. In fact doing this in some form is absolutely essential.

However, the best way of getting people to look at your web site isn't through the Internet at all, but through editorial or advertising in other media. Concoct a story and get press coverage for the launch of your web site. Advertise in the press. Get it reviewed in the magazines read by the people you want to see your site. Oddly enough, these are the ways to get your site visited. Then the visitor numbers will rise, and if you're lucky, will grow on their own.

But give people a reason to visit. They don't want to hear how brilliant you are, they want something from you – even if it's just a good laugh. So your site should contain something useful, too.

On the Internet, newsletters, mailing lists and discussion groups are the best way of spreading the word and keeping people interested. But don't use a spam list with a million names on it. You'll only end up annoying 999,990 of them.

Movies on the Internet

This is slightly off the subject, but I imagine that if you're reading this book, it will be of interest to you. There are two principal problems for independent film and TV producers: the first is getting the programme produced; the second is getting it seen.

The Broadband Internet is on the way, and it's what everyone wants – consumers and content providers. The Broadband Internet will give users data speeds several thousand times the maximum speeds typically available today. It exists in pockets and these islands of connectivity are gradually joining up. It's of interest to producers because it enables various variations on so-called 'video on demand'.

It also enables the development of interactive multimedia experiences which can include theoretically unlimited amounts of full-motion video. DVD has the capacity to do much of this. CD ROM just hasn't got enough room. These technologies have enormous potential, and its going to be interesting how their use develops during the next few years.

The Broadband Internet means that producers can make a film or programmes and sell them through the Internet – the only problem is how you collect the money. There are as many niche-markets as there are customers. In this kind of a world, efficient, high-quality programme-making is even more important.

The script

When asked about the three most important elements in making a good film, Alfred Hitchcock is reputed to have said, 'A good script, a good script – and a good script.'

A script doesn't have to mean the traditional hundred pages or so of action and dialogue of a movie script. A script, in the broadest sense, can be a well-constructed running order on the back of an envelope. The important part of the last sentence is 'well-constructed'.

Efficient programme-making, whether low-budget or not, depends on knowing what you're doing and why you're doing it before you get the expensive toys out of the box. There isn't the time to make things up as you go along. And there isn't the time to shoot all sorts of stuff in the hope of getting a programme out of it later. That wastes time and money, not only on the shoot, but in post-production as well.

That means (once again) spending time in pre-production, where thought and paper are cheap, on developing a solid narrative structure for the series.

In general, drama productions clearly need the script finalized and rehearsed before filming begins. Factual and entertainment programmes clearly can't expect to be scripted to this degree. In fact they should not be scripted to this degree, however tempting it might sometimes be.

In the case of a documentary programme or series, you will have a fairly good idea from your research of what is likely to happen when you film – even if the series is a docu-soap. This is by no means the same as dictating what people say or do. What it means is that the research will be of such quality that the filming produces no major surprises in terms of programme structure. But it's equally important that within the structure there is enough room to handle creatively all the little unexpected nuggets that real life produces for you. Being too rigid will destroy the life – and the credibility – of the programme.

If there is no clearly thought-out structure, the very real danger is that too much useless material is produced, and not enough usable material. It's important to be flexible enough to take advantage of the unexpected, but also to be strong enough to reject temptations which may be pretty, but which are not relevant.

But if you haven't decided what the story is, how are you to know whether something is going to help you tell it, or not? This is important, not only for visual material, but also in deciding the questions and follow-ups to ask in interviews.

Satisfying programmes have a satisfying structure. It has happened (and will continue to happen) that the satisfying structure is developed after filming is complete, but in those cases, post-production tends to be a long, painful, and expensive process. Not to be recommended, and certainly not efficient.

Summary

One of the first things to go when budgets are low is extensive research. Make research efficient and accurate by buying packages of expertise – hire someone who is already an expert.

Make full use of the Internet – but don't believe everything you read, and don't make Internet research a substitute for talking to real people.

Above all, finish the research period with a solid structure to the programme. Once there's a solid structure, everything else falls into place.

CREW AND EQUIPMENT

Now you know what you're going to film. Who is going to film it, and what with?

Equipment

There's a temptation to give a knee-jerk reaction to the words 'low-budget' as follows: if it's a low-budget programme it has to be shot on DV.

DV is a fabulous format (group), and is bringing out a democratization of television and film, and a revolution in working methods arguably greater than the one effected by the introduction of 'lightweight' cameras for ENG use in the mid 1970s.

In that case, the cameras were only lightweight compared to the studio-based, pedestal-based monsters they gradually came to replace almost everywhere. Even the smallest of them was several times heavier and more expensive than the 16 mm cameras which they were working alongside. ENG wasn't even faster. Because of the comparative clumsiness of video editing compared to film, the time saving theoretically available in not having to process the film was eaten up by the extra time it took to edit. Ten minutes of colour reversal film could be processed on a 'desktop processor' in around half an hour and a story cut in ten minutes or so. Linear video editing with slow cassette machines wasn't really faster.

Our subject is cost-efficient programme-making. As we've seen, cutting corners often doesn't save any money. The important thing is to choose the right tools for the job you have to do. That's why our company owns very little equipment. If you own a piece of gear – particularly if it was expensive – you feel bound to use it on everything, even if it isn't really appropriate.

In the case of *Cookery Clinic*, for example, it would have been theoretically possible to have filmed all the programmes on three or four separate DV cameras, and edited the whole show together afterwards. How would that have affected the budget?

The cameras themselves might have been cheaper. However we would still have needed the same crew, so no savings on people. Lighting costs would have been similar. The cost of the OB scanner would have been saved. But editing would have taken a long time – so much more expense there.

It's important to take a holistic view of the production. Many high-end edit suites spend a long time patching up poor-quality work filmed on low-end DV cameras. At, let's say £180 per hour, plus the cost of the director, and possibly a PA and producer, it doesn't take long to negate any cost savings that might have been made through not using a more expensive acquisition medium.

Acquisition formats

The choice of acquisition media for television programmes is wide, and can be confusing. Some decisions will have a fundamental effect on the production's working methods, others change very little.

35 mm film

35 mm film is almost certainly overkill for an essentially television production. However, it is still worth considering as a

possibility, even if it's only to reject it. In the 1960s and '70s many international drama series were filmed on 35 mm. Even now, although it's expensive, it's worth considering for a TV movie with theatrical potential. Filming on 35 mm is also a way of 'future-proofing' your production in readiness for high-definition television, which will come, and will require high-definition programmes.

It's true, however, that 35 mm is unlikely to be the best choice for cost-efficient programme-making without a very strong particular reason.

16 mm film

There is definitely a so-called 'film look'. People can and do argue endlessly about what constitutes this elusive 'film look', and spend ages playing with the set-up on their electronic camera in order to achieve something which satisfies them – at least to an extent.

Part of it, at least, has to do with the definition of film. A PAL television picture has 575 vertical picture lines. That is the maximum resolution that an ordinary PAL signal can achieve, no matter how good the equipment. On a big screen you can see the individual lines with ease. The resolution of film is limited only by the fineness of the grain. That *is* a limitation, to be sure, but the random nature of grain is part of that elusive 'film look', too. Normally, even if it is apparent, it adds to the image rather than detracts from it. However you look at it, 16 mm film is a much higher-definition medium than television.

Another part of this film look has to do with subtlety. The range of shades and the contrast ratio that film can display is much greater than that of video.

All this may be easy to see if you compare a television image side-by-side with a projected film image. The mystery of the whole film look is that you notice it when you run film on television, where the resolution and the subtlety of shades is limited by the television medium. Strange, isn't it?

The full 16 mm film production process, like the choice of 35 mm, is probably one you wouldn't naturally make for a series intended purely for television. But using 16 mm as an acquisition format has several advantages.

16 mm is capable of stunning quality, even on television. The cameras are, in general, considerably smaller and cheaper than their electronic equivalents – although this is less true than it used to be. They are also more robust, and repairs in the field are at least possible. If your Digital Betacam camera breaks down in the middle of the Serengeti, there's absolutely nothing you can do about it. At least you *might* be able to fix a film camera – and you're also more likely to find a repair shop with spares within a reasonable distance.

Another characteristic of film which you don't appreciate until you tasted the freedom, is that the camera and the sound are separate. There's no long wire connecting cameraperson and recordist. They can wander off and do their own thing as long as the slate is on so it can be sorted out later.

These arguments apply equally to Super 16, a wide-screen format which extends the picture area into the edge of the film where one set of sprocket-holes, or a magnetic sound stripe would go.

Super 16 gives you all the advantages of wide-screen, film quality and the flexibility to provide a blow-up to 35 mm for theatrical use if that's the way the production goes.

Whether you shoot standard or Super 16, you would expect to transfer the negative to tape, and perform a non-linear edit just as you would if you'd done the shoot on tape. It's a good compromise. The quality is wonderful, and, if the shooting ratio is kept under control it's surprising how little using film can add to the overall budget – particularly since you save on camera hire costs, and possibly on other incidental expenses such as excess baggage when transporting the kit – because a typical film kit will probably weigh less than the electronic equivalent.

It isn't the lowest budget way of doing things, but this book is about being cost-effective – about producing the best quality result with the most efficient use of resources. Sometimes that is also the lowest budget way of doing it, but not necessarily.

It's certainly true that the cost of using film can quickly get out of hand if you don't keep very tight control of your shooting ratio. The use of tape has engendered habits of just letting the camera run and sorting it all out afterwards. Tape stock is cheap. Working like that won't add much to your production costs – though it can have quite an effect on your post-production budget. But film stock is expensive, particularly by the time you've put it through the processing and telecine process. Also, it tends to come in (roughly) 10 minute rolls, so you can't 'just let it run' for very long. This can be an advantage – in that it helps you to keep the production under control; or it can be a major disadvantage, if the programme's subject really does require the ability to run for long periods of time.

Tape

Betacam SP

Betacam SP became the dominant acquisition and transmission format during the 1990s. I have to say I never really liked it.

Betacam is Sony's way of recycling its failed domestic Betamax format. What would have been a 180 minute cassette in the domestic machine became a 20 minute cassette in a Betacam machine. Of course there's more to it than that, but the underlying technology is the same.

Picture quality can be very good with the right cameras, but it's subjectively slightly inferior to the one-inch studio tape formats it gradually replaced. (In engineering terms it's massively inferior, but what matters is what the pictures look like, not what the numbers say.)

It's strength and its weakness is that it's an analogue format. The range of colours and tones it can reproduce is infinite, where digital technology takes slices. But it's also very vulnerable to damage to the surface of the tape – dropout. It's much more vulnerable than older broadcast tape formats, because so much of the picture is recorded in so little tape area – not only is one field striped diagonally across the tape in one turn of the heads, but the tape itself is so narrow, that any oxide particles that are missing, or which become dislodged, can take with them a significant portion of the picture.

But Betacam SP was the best compromise between quality and usability that there was in the 1990s, and has become a standard by which its successor formats are judged. It's very widespread – universal, in practical terms – and it's basically a robust medium with robust equipment behind it.

But I'm glad to see the back of it, and I wouldn't any more recommend it as a first choice production format.

Digital formats

Digital television has been a long time coming, but it's now well and truly established. A microphone works by converting (transducing) air pressure changes caused by sound waves into electrical signals. A loud noise creates a larger voltage. A higher frequency sound causes the diaphragm in the microphone to vibrate more rapidly, and these changes are recorded, fundamentally, as electrical signals, varying continuously in a way analogous to the original sound.

Digital technology takes slices, or samples, from the information, both in terms of amplitude (how loud it is) and frequency. The idea is that if you have enough samples, the effect will be, to all intents and purposes, continuous. But it never actually is. Digital technology involves some loss of information from the very beginning, which is one reason why there's such a debate about whether CD audio is as good as the best vinyl.

The story of digital television is largely the story of improvements in compression techniques and in the processing power of microchips. Each frame of uncompressed video represents an enormous amount of data to shift, and only relatively recently has the processing power become available to do that at any price, never mind at prices which are within the reach of normal (even broadcast) companies. This data is compressed in various ways to various extents in the different digital video formats. Most compression formats work on the basis that there are only small differences between fields and frames in a scene. If something is moving in front of a background, the background hardly changes from one frame to the next within the scene, so it isn't necessary to record every detail of the background every time.

But this, too, is a swings and roundabouts operation. Not recording redundant data saves on the throughput necessary to tape or disc. But processing the data in real time to work out what is redundant and what is necessary also requires a hefty amount of computing power. A good deal more than was available to send Apollo 11 to the moon in 1969, for one thing.

And all compression leaves signs. It most certainly isn't true that 'digital is digital'. The major advantage of digital video formats is that there is no generation loss in copying them *as long as you are making a true digital copy without decoding and re-encoding the data*. There's a small effective generation loss every time a video signal goes through a codec, but in general it's still more robust than any analogue format.

However there is always a danger in mixing formats. If video is compressed in one format (where a certain amount and type of information is lost) then uncompressed and recompressed in another format (where more 'redundant' information is thrown away, but in a different way) it can lead to some very strange results.

The dangers are not too great if you're careful, but you must be aware of the dangers.

Digital Betacam

Digi-Beta is the standard by which all other digital formats are measured. It's compression ratio is only(!) 2:1; it's expensive. It's very high quality. As the format has become more widespread, so prices have come down towards what used to be the standard for Beta SP not so very long ago – but prices of everything else have dropped even lower, so it's still very much a high-end medium.

It's possible to get high quality results more cheaply, but if the shoot is fairly short, and you have no reason to need smaller gear, then there are arguments for saying Digi-Beta is the default. Use it unless there are reasons not to.

Shooting on Digi-Beta, like shooting on film, does mean that you have to think carefully about exactly how you're intending to go through the post-production process. Do you transfer to a lower cost digital format; or do you go along the 'traditional' off-line/on-line route? Whatever the decision, it can only benefit your production to start off with the highest quality.

D9

D9 began life as Digital-S and is JVC's going it alone bid for a high-end digital format. It became D9 when the technology was ratified as a digital broadcast standard. And they succeeded. In the real world there's very little to choose between D9 and Digital Betacam. Except that the D9 equipment is considerably less expensive. This is helped by the fact that JVC used aggressive pricing as a way of getting the format established against very strong competition from Sony and Panasonic. It's only real problem is that, although it uses VHS-size tapes, in every other respect it's a stand-alone system. You can, of course, copy D9 to other formats, or install a D9 machine in an edit suite, but where Digital Betacam machines will play Beta SP tapes, for example, and DVCPRO machines will play mini-DV and DVCAM tapes, D9 is on its own. Also, the tapes themselves are the largest format in current use.

While there's no question over the quality of the tape format, time will tell whether Digital Betacam maintains its lead in terms of top-end camcorders. The question of the difference between the tape format and the camera is an important one, and one that has greater significance the further down the price ladder you go.

Betacam SX

Betacam SX is Sony's planned digital replacement for Betacam SP. In many ways it's very similar to SP, but uses MPEG2, which also happens to be the standard digital transmission format. However, largely because of the popularity of Digital Betacam, and the way that Digi-Beta's prices have been forced down by a combination of competition and savings of scale through its own success, Betacam SX never really took off.

The DV family

The above formats are all completely different approaches to the problem of digital television, and are not related to each other at all. The DV family of formats, however, all use basically the same way of storing and compressing data. There are minor differences between them, most of which have to do with different approaches to the ruggedness required of professional recordings.

History repeats itself in DV. Back in the 1970s, Umatic was a domestic format which was taken over for professional use. The same thing is happening with DV.

Mini DV was launched firmly as a consumer product. Then programme-makers discovered that a pocket camera with a resolution of around 500 lines for around £1000 could also be used for broadcast television. And the results, while not up to Betacam standards, were certainly better than those produced by tube cameras recording onto Hi-Band Umatic, which was the mainstay of much of European TV news during the early 1980s.

Mini DV has certainly revolutionized a certain kind of pro-gramme making. It's now possible to take a tiny camera, look as if you're a tourist, and practically blend into the background wherever you are. Observational documentaries are able to go places that were scarcely possible before, and they still look (comparatively) wonderful.

Because it is basically a domestic medium, mini DV has a number of reliability problems – tapes recorded on one camcor-der often won't play back on another, for example. And the sound tracks are not really of professional quality. In order to provide something more robust for professional users, Sony and Panasonic separately developed different modifications of the mini DV system. (Sony also introduced another digital format, Digital 8, which is still basically the mini DV format in an 8 mm tape cassette, and plays Video 8 and Hi-8 tapes, too.)

Sony's DVCAM uses a larger tape, which runs at a higher speed, with only two higher-quality audio tracks. DVCAM camcorders and VCRs will play mini DV tapes, but won't record on them. Some DVCAM decks will play DVCPRO tapes.

Panasonic's DVCPRO uses an even larger tape, and samples the colour differently. DVCPRO decks will play DVCAM and mini DV tapes.

With their improved robustness and higher quality sound, either of these are as good *as a tape format* as Betacam SP. That emphasis is important, particularly in the world of cost-effective programme-making. The arrival of DV represents a true revolution in television. It brings with it a democratization of technology similar to the arrival of desktop publishing on the home and office computer.

And, in a very similar way, DV technology is being abused on a daily basis. 'DV' has become synonymous with researchers or directors taking £1000 cameras and filming 'reality' footage. There's no doubt that the availability of cameras this small, which are capable of producing footage of this quality, has produced a true revolution in production for certain kinds of programming.

But – and this is an important 'but' – it is naive to expect a camera costing £1000 to rival the performance of a camera costing £30,000 or more, where the lens alone accounts for nearly half the price of the camera. *As a tape format* the DV family is capable of results rivalling Betacam SP. But cheap cameras are cheap cameras however you look at it, and the use of cheap cameras, often, it has to be said, wielded without skill, has given DV something of a undeservedly bad reputation.

The manufacturers themselves are beginning to realize this, and are beginning to produce DV-based cameras clearly aimed at the professional and broadcast markets. Panasonic has always aimed DVCPRO at this market. Sony has become more aggressive with its DVCAM equipment – and its introduction of Digital 8 could be seen as a way of attempting to remove DV from the consumer market altogether.

It was very interesting that when I first went to discuss the co-production of our *Cafés* series with Wien 1, they were about to move and totally re-equip their studio. At that time, the head of production (who had previously been the head of television engineering for the whole of the ORF, Austria's national broadcaster) was talking about Digital Betacam. When we went back to edit a few months later, the move was complete, and the entire station was using DVCPRO. They obviously considered the quality more than adequate.

What does it all mean? That I have no hesitation in using DVCAM or DVCPRO for production – but I would only use cameras at the consumer end of the market as a backup, or where the fact that they are so small and unobtrusive gives you important production advantages.

You do need to be aware when making this decision that the DV family is a comparatively 'lossy' way of recording colour information. For normal use, and basic processing – such as titles, fades, mixes, simple copies – that isn't a problem; but, although you might get away with it, it's better not to try using it for work involving multi-layered effects, or chroma-key.

DVCPRO 50

I've left DVCPRO 50 to the end, but, really it belongs with D9 and Digital Betacam. DVCPRO 50 is Panasonic's upgrading of the DVCPRO format to compete with these other two formats, and there isn't much to choose between them. They are all three capable of producing the highest quality results with the right cameras.

There are always going to be improvements in technology, and there will always be local reasons to prefer one format over another – whether it's personal preference, or the availability of a certain kind of equipment. In general, although there are several formats to choose from, the choice of production format should never be made on equipment cost alone. Think about the whole production. Consider how you're going to edit the programme before you make the final decision on acquisition format, and always use the highest quality camera you can afford.

One of the best reasons for using the DV family is the availability of desk-top editing: a broadcast quality edit suite on a Mac or PC. More of this later.

Single or multi-camera

Some people in television don't consider anything to be real television unless it's live. If it can't be live, then it should be recorded multi-camera as if it were live.

Some kinds of show are always recorded in a multi-camera studio: game-shows; chat-shows. Usually it's obvious why shows are produced in the way they've always been produced, and it would be simply perverse to try to do them any other way. But not always.

Multi-camera production is always more expensive per production hour than single-camera shooting because you're using more people and more equipment. Multi-camera production has its roots in live television: if something is happening only once you have to be sure that you can cover it from all necessary angles – and make it interesting to look at. It's typically suited to factory-style environments, where there's a high throughput of programming, because the set-up costs tend to be high. A set has to be built and lit.

One of the main disadvantages is that a set has to be lit for all camera angles at once.

The main advantage of multi-camera studio television is that a lot of programming can be produced very quickly. Typically two, three, or even four half-hour game shows might be produced in a single day. And these benefits can often be gained outside the studio, too, by producing with a multi-camera outside broadcast (OB) set-up.

There are two reasons why you would make the decision to use multi-camera techniques: the first, and main reason is because you need to produce a lot of programmes in a short time, where the programmes are, like game shows, very similar in format. The other reason is if, as in sport (or real live shows) the event you're filming is going to happen only once.

Although the hourly cost of multi-camera production is considerably higher than working with a single camera, the overall cost to the production need not be higher, since you should be saving a great deal on edit costs.

The worst of all worlds is where a long time is spent in an expensive studio, and then a long time is needed in the edit suite afterwards, as well. In cost-efficient programme production this mustn't be allowed to happen.

Crew

You might have decided what your acquisition format is going to be – who's going to drive the equipment?

The first fundamental decision to make is how much you are going to pay people. The best people are expensive – everyone charges what they think they can get out of the market, and the best people can demand higher prices from the market (largely) because the market thinks that these people are worth the extra money.

They're worth the extra money because they're particularly good at their job, certainly, but not everyone is outstanding in the same way. Some people are in demand because they have brilliant ideas; others because they're very fast; some cameramen are wonderful at action shoots and useless with people; some are wonderful at lighting but no good with sport.

In every production, you need to analyse the needs of the programme production process, and be clear about what skills will help you most. Whether the decision is to go for expensive crew members or not, the people who are on the crew must be people whose talents are suited to the series being produced.

That isn't the same as saying, 'You've never done drama, or dance, or sport, so you can't do this show.' but it is important to make sure that the crew are in sympathy with the production. Programme-making is not usually a democratic process, but it is most certainly a collaborative process. It is not possible to understate the importance of *every* crew member to the success of a production. 'Even' a runner arriving not caring that she or he turns up late with extra stock, or gaffer tape, or whatever, could hold up the production (which costs money) and sour the mood of everyone (which costs money and affects the quality of the work).

The three most important people in the actual production of a programme are the director, the cameraperson, and the editor. The two of those who have most influence on the final quality of the programme or series are the cameraperson and the editor. (With apologies to sound recordists everywhere. I'll make up for it further on.)

So what do you get when you pay top prices? You'd expect to get someone who's very good at what they do, but are they good in the way you need? In our kind of programme-making we need someone who is very good, very quickly – not the person who is absolutely brilliant, but takes all day.

Every production is a prototype, but some problems occur again and again with only small variations. The advantage of more experienced crew is that they will have encountered a similar problem before, and will also have been through most of the possible solutions. Less experienced people may need to spend more time trying things out.

You could expect the more experienced crew member to produce more consistent results – which should mean you have to worry less about doing things basically for insurance reasons – in case one of the other shots didn't work. Having said all that, the last thing you want is a grumpy old man who thinks he's seen it all before and done it all before and always knows better.

What happens if you decide to pay less, and employ less well experienced people? Possibly you get exactly the results you need. Some people seem able just to turn on and do brilliantly right from the beginning. More likely, in all honesty, is that things will take longer. Certainly you, the producer, will have to be more careful to be aware of everything that's going on. I'd be inclined to give everyone the opportunity to learn, and to gain from the experience of others by finding truly experienced people to be camera-people, sound recordist, editor. With most other jobs you get a second chance if something goes awry without putting the whole schedule in jeopardy. Very often there won't be anything you can pin down, but at the end of the day, everything just seems to have taken longer.

Do not misunderstand me. I don't mean to imply that beginners are dangerous. But I don't agree with some companies' ways of exploiting newcomers in the name of career development by throwing them in at the deep end and expecting them to swim with only the most basic training, and without giving them time to train themselves – and paying them peanuts, which is really why it happens. This is some companies' way of making low-budget programmes, and in general it results in a lot of not very good material.

Far better, I would have thought, to have a mixed crew, led by people who can train at least by example. And I speak from experience when I say that working with the kind of people I'm talking about is like drawing back the curtains on a whole new world after working with people who are simply competent.

These decisions are similar but different on a large-budget production where there is more room to manoeuvre. In our kind of programme-making we have to be efficient – meaning not only good, but fast, too. That's the only way to make good programmes and a profit when budgets are being pared down to the minimum.

Ultimately the best policy is to do yourself a favour and complement the skills you have by making sure that the people who are doing things you're not so good at are in a position to make a significant contribution to the series. You hope to get something extra from colleagues, something you hadn't already thought of. Take chances from a position of strength, not from a position of weakness.

How many people do you need?

You need as many people as it takes to do the job. No more, and certainly no fewer. While I don't think many people yearn for the Good Old Days when you had an electrician for every lamp, and every crew seemed to have fifty people doing something or other, you can certainly go too far in reducing numbers. Two-person crews (camera and sound) are routinely asked to do too much, because it's cheaper to hire two people than three. But it also takes longer for them to get the work done. And it doesn't really make sense for a highly qualified, experienced cameraperson to spend half the day wrapping cables and carrying boxes.

Usually, adding a third person – probably an electrician – can speed things up considerably. You'll find you're able to achieve far more each day without exhausting everyone.

And this holds true all the way through the list of possible crew. If sound is important, you need someone to swing the boom. If you need make-up, one person may be enough, but don't ask her or him to do make-up on whole crowds on their own, while the rest of the crew are paid to stand around.

Crewing up

Everybody develops their own short list of people they call first. The way to find the right people for your series if you don't already know them, or if the people you do know are not available is, quite honestly, to ask around. Most work in our business is found through personal recommendation. Advertising is expensive, unreliable, and time-consuming. It's much quicker to call or visit a few production managers in other production companies, or talk to people at crewing companies and facilities houses. Once you've talked to three or four different people you'll almost certainly find that the same names keep coming up again and again. This is true wherever in the world you are. Ours is always a small industry where most of the players know each other.

You can make life a bit easier for yourself by concerning yourself only with hiring your heads of department: camera, sound, design. Let them hire their assistants – with your approval, of course, because you'll be paying the bill. But, all other things being equal, it's more important for the sound recordist and the sound assistant to work well together as a team, than for the producer to enjoy the company of the sound assistant. Obviously you don't want any friction, but friction is rare in a well-managed unit. Freelancers have to get on with everyone, or they don't work.

Summary

- ❏ Choose the highest quality acquisition format that you can afford. Equipment hire costs make less difference than you think.
- ❏ Think of DV as a tape format, not as a camera collection.
- ❏ Hire the best people.
- ❏ But people, format, equipment must be the right choice for the programme.
- ❏ Always consider the whole production process when making these decisions, don't simply count the money going out of the door on any given day in isolation.

OVERSEAS PRODUCTION

Traditional wisdom has it that low budget television has to be produced within thirty miles of your base. In a world where travelling any further meant having to pay for fares, hotels, and meals for a large crew, all of whom came along, that's true. But we, who work in smaller units with greater flexibility, don't have such problems.

The opposite extreme of transporting a whole crew with all its equipment, is to send just a director and hire a local crew wherever it is you need to film. This can work well if you are the producer/director going to a country you know, where language isn't a problem; or if all you need is a few shots or an interview. It can be very risky if you need more from the shoot, if only because the director is unsupported, a long way from the production base, and if something goes wrong it's going to be difficult to sort out quickly. There may be no danger except to the budget and schedule, but it's precisely that that we're trying to keep under control, here.

Case history: *Cafés of Europe*

Clearly we couldn't film a series on Cafés in Europe within thirty miles of London. Equally, on £25,000 there was a limit to how many places we could go. Although the ideal would probably have been to visit six cities – one for each programme – that didn't seem a very practical idea, either. We would have spent too much time travelling, and not enough filming.

So we decided to choose three cities and do two programmes in each city. We'd divide the programmes up so that the first one would have an

(a)

(b)

(c)

Figure 7.1 Travel is possible on low budgets. Madrid (a) and at the Wailing Wall in Jerusalem (b and c).

introduction to the city, and would feature the biggest and most famous establishments. The second programme would discover secret places that only the residents would normally know about. In this way we managed to make a virtue out of our very real budget limitations, and concentrate both the filming and the travelling as much as possible.

Obviously you have to film in Paris if you're making a series about café life. As it happens, I know Vienna very well, and I don't believe you can ignore Vienna. The third city we chose was Madrid, because our presenter knew the city well.

Since the basic research had already been done for the production of the book, we needed only a local fixer to go around a long short-list of establishments to find out if they were prepared to take part in the series. I then travelled out, as producer-director, with our production assistant and the presenter a couple of days before we filmed, so that we could make the final decision on where we were going to film. So each pair of programmes involved only one set of fares.

Local crews

Our overall schedule was fixed by the budget, too. We had to film for each pair of programmes in three days. We asked amongst our colleagues and followed up recommendations for local crews in Paris and Madrid (I knew people in Vienna already). Since we knew that there wouldn't be time to do any but the most basic lighting, we booked a two-man crew in each place.

Using local crews whom you don't know is a risk. You can't be sure of what you're going to get, and, although the industry works in pretty similar ways around the world, there are always going to be differences in attitudes and expectations. On the other hand, these differences are probably usually no greater than the differences between working with a crew whose members have been inside, say the BBC, all their working lives, and a crew who have always been freelance.

One major advantage you do get with a local crew is just that – they are local. You can take advantage of their local knowledge and experience. They know whether or not you need permits or can get away with just filming anyway. They know how to handle the policeman who strolls up through the middle of your shot. They know the way around, so you don't spend that vital hour or two just simply lost.

And they know the best places to go in the evening after you've finished. If you deal with a local crew, you might be able to get away without having to employ a local fixer separately. If you bring your crew with you, you will almost always need to have someone locally to set things up for you – otherwise you risk arriving with your expensive crew and equipment, and being unable to get to work because some vital permit is missing, or there was a misunderstanding about the day of your arrival.

In the event, our cafés filming worked out very well, although there were one or two worrying moments. In particular the first morning's filming in one of the cities seemed to take forever. If we hadn't begun to work faster, we would have been lucky to have covered half the scheduled work in the three days. Luckily the reason seemed to be that the cameraman was trying to impress with his thoroughness, and proved perfectly capable of doubling his speed and still getting pictures that were just as good. It was an interesting couple of hours, though, and a reminder of what a knife edge the success of the whole enterprise was balanced on.

Case history: *Free at Last*

A few years ago we made a film (16 mm) with Amnesty International, which involved filming literally all around the world. I travelled with a Production Assistant, and we hired local crews in the places we were filming in.

The routeing on our ticket was so complicated that when we wanted to change one of the flights in Miami, we had to buy another ticket and reclaim the money later, because nobody at Miami was able to recalculate the fare.

We actually filmed in Tokyo, Nagasaki, Santo Domingo, Lima, San Francisco, Copenhagen, Madrid, and London; and the schedule was very tight. The whole trip was done in a month. We were surprised at how low the total hotel costs were, until we realized that we'd spent nearly as many nights on aircraft as in hotels. It worked, but I'm not sure I'd like to repeat the experience in exactly the same way.

In particular, we booked most of the crews through the London news agencies, Visnews and UPITN. This made life easier for us, but meant that what we had were people used to filming news. There are advantages to this: crews are used to working quickly, and to finding their way around with a minimum of fuss. They are also very good at getting you in and out of places without fuss – Amnesty International was not exactly a popular organization in Peru in those days.

However, the first concern of news crews is, quite rightly, to get the pictures and get them back to the newsroom. Some camera and sound crews who are used to working mainly in news are not the kind of people you'd choose if you want good-looking pictures. They're accustomed to following action, not to painting with light. Quality can be very variable. You have to be careful that you are aware of everything that's going on, to make sure that you get the results you need. In one case, too, our cameraman had become so used to ENG cameras that he'd all but forgotten how to light for film.

Another disadvantage of working in this way is that you have eight different cameramen on a single film. In this case, that was not so much of a concern, because a large proportion of our programme was composed of archive news footage, but it is certainly an important consideration for more 'normal' programmes.

A compromise which has often worked well is to take the series lighting cameraperson with you, but hire equipment, recordist, and any other crew locally. This gains you a double benefit: you achieve a consistent 'look' through the series, together with a cameraperson you know you can rely on; and you still have the advantages of local knowledge from the rest of the crew. You do have to be careful of language problems in this case, which make it difficult for your cameraperson to work with the rest of the crew. At the least, you are likely to find that work goes more slowly than you might hope.

Production assistant

Different people work in different ways. Very often the PA is the first crew member to be dropped, in order to bring the budget down.

Personally, I prefer not to do without a PA, because on my productions, the PA is much more than just a note-taker. Particularly on smaller productions, I like to work together with the PA as a production team. Of course, the producer always has to make the final decision, but otherwise we set everything up together; the PA knows everything I know, and is equipped, and qualified to sort out many problems without my even knowing they've arisen. This kind of approach allows the producer/ director to be almost in two places at once. Interviewees and locations can be prepared two steps ahead of the filming. Problems can be solved without interrupting the filming. And the PA offers another, friendly, point of view with whom to discuss things.

Treated in this way, the PA is a vital team member, who improves the efficiency of the whole production. I quite agree, though, that there's no point in taking someone along at the expense of extra salary, fares and hotels, if all they do is write down timecodes.

Air fares

Rule number one: never pay full price for anything. Rule number two: don't be mean.

❑ **Rule One:** It's well known that two people sitting in neighbouring seats on flights can be paying widely different fares for the same journey. It's your task as producer to ensure that the fares you pay for are at the lower end of the range.

You can waste a lot of time calling round every travel agent who advertises in the back of the weekend papers, or the London *Evening Standard*. I can promise you now that most of them are either offering standard APEX fares, or spare seats on charter flights and that most of the low prices they advertise are only theoretically available – perhaps they once had a seat on an otherwise full flight which they sold at that price.

Similarly, trawling cheap flight sites on the Internet can be useful in giving you an idea of what you ought to be able to get the ticket for, but many of the flights you'll be offered have so many conditions attached to them that it isn't practical to use them for production travel.

Of course you can find bargains this way, but very often you may find that the few pounds you save aren't really worth the effort it took to save them.

The practical answer is to try out a few travel agents (on the Internet and on the telephone) with a few likely routes, and settle on two or maybe three travel agents that you can trust to do you a good deal. Let them do the work for you. That's what they're for. Good travel agents tend to specialize in certain areas of types of travel; and if you use the same people repeatedly, you should find that they try a little bit harder for you. But find a travel agent who is used to business travel; you don't want a holiday shop. And it very rarely makes sense to go direct to the airlines: they'll only sell to you at the official rates.

APEX fares nearly always involve a minimum Saturday night stay, because they're intended to encourage people to travel when the lucrative business travellers want to stay at home. These fares are much cheaper than the standard return fares. But don't forget that you'll have to pay for probably an extra two night's hotels and meals, so they may not save the overall budget very much in the end. And if you want to change the booking later, you'll have to pay at least the difference between the cheap fare and the full price fare for the changed leg.

Some routes have low fares with a minimum two nights stay, but can be used during the week. And if airlines are trying to establish themselves on routes they may offer very low fares with no conditions. For example, the cheapest way to Montreal from London might be via Paris.

Get the airlines to pay

You have to be careful about how many sponsorship or product placement rules you might be breaking, but if you agree to show the airline's aircraft in your programmes, and if they will be seen by a market that the airline is interested in, you might be able to persuade the airline to transport you for nothing.

There'll be much less of a problem in this respect if your series is being produced without a commission from a UK broadcaster. Most other countries take a much more relaxed attitude to sponsorship in its various forms. Once the series is complete, it can still be sold into the UK, and no questions will be asked.

We once produced a series which was most definitely sponsored, in a way which wouldn't have been allowed under the rules of the time. We've sold it several times to various channels in the UK. The only time anyone objected was when the BBC thought that a supermarket was too prominently featured, and wouldn't show that episode, even though the supermarket was sponsoring an event that we were covering. Ironically the supermarket had absolutely nothing to do with our programme.

Air charter

You can also hire a whole aircraft – and still save money. Under certain conditions, your production can benefit greatly from chartering a small aircraft to take you where you want to go, when you want to go. I've done it several times.

One production had a very tight schedule, involving filming in London, Newcastle, North Wales, and Oxford all in the same week. We chartered an 8-seater aircraft from Blackbushe, a smaller airfield in the south, and did all the filming as day trips. Journey time was around an hour and a half each way, so we were able to get a full day's filming and be back at a sensible time each night.

Firstly, this schedule would not have been possible any other way (except possibly by spending most of every night on the road). Secondly, even if the schedule had not been a problem, several days' travel time would have to have been paid for, as would overnight hotels. The aircraft charter cost less than that alternative.

Additionally, such smaller aircraft can use smaller airfields, which are very often much closer to your final destination than the major airports (which you can use as well, if you need to). There are hundreds of often very busy smaller airfields across Europe and North America. Even in the UK. Also, you're not tied to airline schedules. You fly when you're ready.

Charter operators will be reluctant to give you general rules, but will happily quote for a specific flight. As a rough guide, this kind of aircraft (something like a Piper Navajo or Aztec, or a Cessna 300 or 400 series) will fly at around 200 miles per hour, and will cost you something like £400 per flying hour. A day trip to Hull or Amsterdam from the south of England might cost a bit under £1000. The alternative is at least one travel day and one night in a hotel for the crew – roughly the same, even if the schedule isn't a problem. In the Amsterdam example, the price of charter is about the same as four standard fares. Take a fifth person and your gear and you save money.

The sums work out well for journeys of up to about 500 miles: Cologne, Lyon, Copenhagen, from the south of England. It's not the answer to everything, but it's a serious alternative solution to some programme problems.

Hotels and car hire

The rules about not paying full price apply even more strongly in the case of car hire, and particularly, hotels. Nearly all car-hire and hotel chains have so-called 'corporate' rates. Membership of almost any organization will give the establishments enough reason to give you these rates, which can be 50 per cent or more off the prices you see pinned up in the foyer. Of course your travel agent will be doing all this for you, and probably have their own deals to pass on, but be sure that you're getting the benefit of them.

If you are booking direct, you can normally think of a reason why they should give you a discount. For instance, if you're travelling with a crew: five people for three or four nights is a lot of rooms. That deserves a deal. If you should be in the unfortunate position of arriving somewhere late in the afternoon without having rooms booked, you should also be able to get discount. If the rooms aren't sold by now, they're just wasted space. Any cash is better than nothing to the hotel.

❑ **Rule Two:** A happy crew is an efficient crew. If you don't believe in keeping people happy out of the goodness of your heart, then do it to benefit the budget. Grumpy people don't work as well as happy people.

It is always possible, if you try hard enough, to get a room somewhere for less than you're paying; but it isn't worth it. The few pounds you save will be lost in wasted time the next day. There's nothing more miserable than having a hard day's work and then arriving at a doss-house of a hotel where the roof leaks and they ask you to pay before you go to bed. This is not to say that a crew should be cosseted with palatial surroundings and £500 per night suites; but a comfortable room in a reasonably pleasant hotel can make a great deal of difference.

The object is to make high quality programmes on low budgets. Some production companies take the attitude that every penny spent on the production is a penny taken away from the company's profits. If you take that to its logical conclusion, how do any programmes get made? Companies have to make profits, or they can't survive until the next production. But anyone who is in this business to make a fortune is in the wrong business and should leave straight away. How much better to make good programmes in a happy environment with people you enjoy working with? It can be done.

Summary

❏ Overseas production will always be more expensive than staying close to your base, but it can be done efficiently at surprisingly little extra cost.

❏ Try to get personal recommendations for local overseas crews.

❏ Local crews provide local knowledge, and often make the expense of a separate fixer unnecessary.

❏ A good and safer compromise is to take your own cameraperson with you and hire the rest of the crew and the gear at your destination.

❏ Never pay full price for air travel, hotels or vehicle hire. There's always a discount to be had.

❏ A few pennies extra on a comfortable bed makes virtually no difference to your budget, but keeps everyone happy – and working more efficiently.

CHAPTER 8 — PRODUCTION SCHEDULING

You have your subject. You know who is going to be filming it, and generally where it's all going to happen. Now you have to work out the best order to do things in so that your production stands the biggest chance of finishing on schedule – because over-schedule almost always means over-budget, and we can't afford that.

Putting together a production schedule is always something of a juggling exercise. There's an ideal order to do things in. And then there's the way you do it in the end, because someone is only available at a certain time, or you can only film in Brighton Pavilion between midnight and 4 a.m., and so on.

I think the single most important suggestion I have to make is that you always build contingency into the schedule in exactly the same way as a well-constructed budget not only has a general contingency, but also areas within the line items which give you room to breathe.

In the case of a schedule I have two concrete suggestions for helping your budget. The first is to schedule all your exteriors first. Not so important in the Caribbean, perhaps, but in Britain, the chances of the weather ruining your minutely worked-out plans are extremely high. If you have all the exteriors scheduled at the beginning and you manage to get them all in, that's absolutely wonderful. If, which is far more likely, it rains so hard you can't see across the street on an exterior day, then you've still got plenty of other stuff to be getting on with. Just pull forward one of the interior shoots, and re-schedule the exterior. The missing exterior day then has no effect on the overall schedule. (You will, of course, already have possible interior scenes set up so that it's possible to change your plans at the last minute like this with only a minimum loss of time.) If you leave all the exteriors to the end, and it rains on you, then, of course, you go over schedule, and over-budget. Weather insurance is expensive. You may end up having to pay for the extra day or days yourself.

This is a sensible basic plan for filming of any sort that involves going outdoors. Of course there are times when you can't do the ideal thing. Some shoots or events take place entirely out of doors. But it's still a useful way to start thinking about the schedule.

Secondly, plan to start with something easy. Every production has in it scenes which could be a bit of a problem – where everyone is glad when they're over – and others which are straightforward. If you start with something straightforward – just for the first half-day or so – then it gives everyone time to settle down, and for the production team to begin to develop a routine and turn into the 'machine' that gets on with things.

That just leaves everything else. The longest journey begins with a single step. Whether the production is very simple, or much more complex, the basic shopping list still applies: what's being filmed; who's behind the camera; who's in front of the camera; what else needs to be there – set, props, and so on; where is it all happening?

The aim of any efficient schedule is to group things together so that you spend as little time as possible setting up, striking, or moving between locations. This applies equally to the smallest documentary, and the biggest drama. The difference is, the larger the crew, the longer it takes even to move half a mile down the road.

Script breakdown

Any production schedule needs to be preceded by a breakdown of the script or running order so that you can make a list of who and what is needed in every location – or every scene. There's nothing magical about doing a breakdown. It's the same old shopping list: who, what, where.

What you do have to decide is how long it's going to take to do each scene, or section. This is a lot easier for a producer/director to do, because she or he doesn't have to double-guess someone else's preferences. However you do it, it must be realistic. And everyone involved must be happy that your plans are possible. In particular that means the director (if it's not you), and whoever the lighting cameraperson is. After all, lighting is going to take a significant part of the overall production time. The person who's doing it needs to be confident that they have enough time.

So don't fool yourself, and don't crowd people into corners – it's better to finish early than to go over. But, obviously, everyone has to be aware that the schedule is going to be tight.

Most important is to keep the schedule under control. However complex the production is, your schedule will be put together from quite small building blocks. And it's these building blocks that you have to look to. Do that, and everything stays together. Productions that start going wrong at the beginning very rarely make it to the end within the original schedule.

Think in half-days at this stage. If you have scheduled to work into the evening, divide the day into three. And be realistic about what you can achieve in each half-day. I repeat myself, but don't fool yourself; it will only lead to unhappiness and loss of money. The desired end result is efficiency, not slavery – and not programmes that are unwatchable because it was impossible for the crew to do anything properly in the time available.

Case history: Studio (*Cookery Clinic*)

Cookery Clinic was a series of eight one-hour programmes recorded 'as live'. An early decision was to do two programmes a day – but not three. It's not a problem to produce three or even four fairly simple half-hour game shows a day where the programme format is rigid. Not only were our programmes longer (actually the running time was practically the same as four half-hour game shows), but they were more demanding. The format was set, but quite what was going to happen within each section was in the hands of the audience and of the presenter – who, consequently, was under a great deal of pressure to keep things moving and interesting. For that reason alone, we felt it was impractical to drive him any harder. A day's third show would not have been a good one.

Similarly, we were fortunate in being able to build in some breathing space. Two shows a day were recorded, on days one, three, five and six. That is, after the first and second days, we built in a day to reset, reconsider (if necessary) and prepare properly for the next programmes. By the time we got to the second half – the last four programmes – we felt comfortable that we would be working well enough to go straight through.

The shows were recorded, as you might expect, one finishing before the lunch break, and one finishing by the end of the afternoon. That was logical in this case, but it's also a possibility (depending on the nature of the shows) to rehearse all day and record everything in one block. That means, for example, that in a studio situation the record VTR wouldn't be needed until quite late in the day.

In the event, our crew arrived by 08:30 every day, and had their coats on to depart by 18:00, by which time we had two complete programmes in the can.

Case history: Travel documentary (*Cafés of Europe*)

Cafés of Europe was budgeted for a three-day shoot in each of three cities. Material for two 25 minute programmes had to be produced in those three days, with one crew and one camera.

The series is a travel guide to cafés, so the decision on what to film was reasonably straightforward. In each establishment we needed a combination of interviews, architectural shots, and just shots of people going about their daily business. We were, in any case, going to be at the mercy of whoever happened to be there at the time, but an essential part of the planning process was to discover at what time of day each of our cafés was busiest – packed at breakfast and empty in the evening, or vice versa. I though we could reasonably expect to get through our shopping list for each establishment in about two hours, provided that our lighting was kept to a minimum. The days were divided, in this case, into four blocks of two hours, and locations scheduled accordingly.

Since the air fares were cheaper if we returned to London each time – making three separate trips, rather than one longer round trip – each city was contained within a week, with filming on Tuesday to Thursday. Although we used local crews, the production was saved the expense of putting up the director, PA, and presenter in hotels over two weekends. Again, in the event it worked out very well, but it's easy to see what a domino effect could result if the whole thing had begun to slide.

Case history: Drama (*The Chef's Apprentice*)

The Chef's Apprentice was a much bigger production, but still produced very efficiently for costume drama. If a drama script is laid out in the conventional manner, each page of script tends to represent *on average* about a minute of screen time. It's usual when scheduling drama to start from a number of pages to cover in a day. It's a good place to start, but obviously it can be rather dangerous if that's as far as it goes.

It's clear that an action scene, which might be described in three lines in the script, might take two days to shoot, and a simple two-handed dialogue scene might go on for several pages, but be covered in a couple of hours. The kind of thing that is less clear is that some scenes are just harder to stage than others. It's important to think about the content of the scenes when scheduling. How much time they need to set up, possibly even their importance to the plot.

If the production is to make the most efficient use of time, then somebody (producer and/or director) needs to go through the schedule projecting themselves forward in time and considering in detail what needs to go into each scene. That's the kind of thing that isn't so necessary when there's plenty of time – over a long schedule, the swings and roundabouts effect will see everything all right in the end. But when time is very tight, and we're talking about scheduling each hour, someone needs to put this level of thought into it. Because time spent thinking costs virtually nothing early on, before it all starts, but becomes very expensive later on.

Family Affairs, a Channel 5 soap, works out how long they think each scene is going to take to record, and schedules accordingly – although the actors aren't allowed to see this detailed schedule, in case they decide to take the morning off because they're not expected to be needed until after lunch.

The Chef's Apprentice was a drama-doc series of six half-hour programmes. Each episode was a separate drama, topped and tailed with a presenter's piece to camera, and an interview.

The drama was scheduled for a four-day shoot (at 5 to 6 minutes a day) from Monday to Thursday, with Friday set for the 'documentary' pieces and as a reserve day for the drama. All the preparation for the whole series was done in the single pre-production period, but there were two director/PA teams, each doing alternating programmes with the same crew, so that final preparations could continue at the same time as filming was going on.

This was necessary because each week was set in a completely different period, and often in a completely different location:

Week One: Roman Britain, Hever Castle, Kent
Week Two: Renaissance Italy, Hever Castle, Kent
Week Three: Medieval Britain, Penshurst Place, Kent; and Cowdray Park, Sussex
Week Four: Seventeenth century France, Longleat House, Wiltshire
Week Five: Regency Britain, Brighton Pavilion
Week Six: Paris 1900, central London

This was not a low-cost production, but even so, to bring in a half-hour period drama (filmed and delivered on 16 mm) for around £125,000 with a crew of 60, and casts of 20 actors and up to 100 extras still counts as efficient programme-making.

Directors all have their own attitudes to rehearsal. If what you're producing is basically a single-camera movie, then you have a choice about whether to rehearse beforehand or whether to do most of your rehearsal on set. If you need to stick to a short production schedule with little room for manoeuvre, you don't really have a choice. Successful efficient programme-making requires every stage of the work to be carried out involving only those people who are absolutely necessary. Otherwise you're just paying people to wait around while others work. That's part of programme-making, I know, but the trick is to keep to a minimum the people waiting for their turn to work. To have a whole crew standing around while you rehearse is something you can't afford.

Rehearse while the scene is being lit, yes, (though not on the set when lamps and cables are being moved around) but these rehearsals should be refinements to performance and blocking – not starting from scratch and hoping that the artists have learnt their words.

Alternatives

The preceding suggestions have all assumed that the production takes the route of engaging crew and cast who may be expensive, but who will be experienced enough to work reliably and rapidly to fit in with a tight schedule. In that case, the tighter the schedule, the more important it is that everyone involved is aware of the pressures, and happy that they are able to deliver what's needed.

However, if you have decided to pay lower fees because your team is less experienced, the production period will almost certainly be longer. Certainly it would be sensible to allow more flexibility in the schedule in case it takes longer to get the results you need.

However you choose your crew, there's no substitute for developing a programme properly before you begin production. Once the machine has started it's too late. I know how tempting it is to promise to yourself that details will be adjusted or amended later on. In practice what tends to happen is that early decisions stick. So it's best to make sure that they are good ones.

Low-budget programme production has a bad reputation, because it is often produced by producers who exploit people by paying next to nothing and demanding the production of vast amounts of programming. The crews may be very talented, but they're not given time to develop their skills in a constructive way. At its worst this attitude leads to a lazy and uncertain packaging of stale ideas, because nobody has time to stop and think of a more interesting way of working.

Summary

- ❏ Be realistic in the schedule – how long is it really going to take?
- ❏ Break it down into small chunks, so that you don't lose control of it.
- ❏ Start on the first day with something easy to get everyone working together.
- ❏ Schedule the areas you have least control over at the beginning of the shoot, so that if they go wrong, or it rains, you can move something else up and try again while still staying within your overall schedule.
- ❏ Working lots of overtime is not normally better than lengthening the production period. People get tired, and it doesn't save any money overall.

CHAPTER 9

PRODUCTION

So far most of the discussion has really been aimed at the producer. The producer's job is to get the right people in the right place with the right script. Once filming or recording begins, it's the director's job to deliver the pictures to the required standard, within the required schedule.

It's often said that a director's job is '90 per cent perspiration and 10 per cent inspiration'. Certainly the director in the earlier days of Hollywood was treated as a technician like any other. 'You say "Action",' an actor told King Vidor on his first day on set as a director, 'and we start acting. And when we're done acting, you say "Cut".'

The director's position is a little like that of an orchestral conductor, and the ways in which directors work are just as varied as those of conductors. However you choose to do it, the director's job is to encourage other people to do what they do best, in a way which fits together in the best way for the production, both artistically, and purely managerially.

To direct is to channel; to nudge everyone's contribution in the same direction to the same destination. It's a bit like being the best kind of host at a party, where everyone feels that they are enjoying themselves in their own way, but the host is still shaping the whole event in ways which pass unnoticed at the time. Directors (unless they do something else, like operate the camera) don't actually *do* anything. They just show and tell. Informed by their unique personal vision, if you like, but show and tell none the less.

It used to be a chic thing to do to hire the Vienna Philharmonic Orchestra for a private concert where the host – a prominent banker in Vienna, for example – would show off in front of all his friends and cronies by conducting. The orchestra's leader was once asked what really happened in occasions like that.

'Well,' he said, 'it all depends. If they treat us well, we give them von Karajan. If they're OK, but not so friendly, we'll give them someone not so good.'

'And what if they try to push you around?'

The leader shrugs, 'Then we do what they tell us. Serves them right.'

Good cast and crew don't need a director to tell them how to do their jobs. A good director encourages people to give their best. The director is there to make sure it all fits together, and that it happens on time.

Daily schedules

As director, you will have agreed the daily schedule, and you will have decided how you intend to shoot each scene, and developed a much more detailed shopping list for yourself of the shots you need.

If you're sensible this list will be further subdivided into shots which are absolutely essential or there's no programme, and shots which would be nice if there's time. That preparation gives you the breathing space to adjust the schedule as you go to take advantage of – or minimize the influence of – the unexpected.

The management part of the director's job involves constantly evaluating and re-evaluating the schedule, the amount that has been covered, and the amount still to be covered. It's part of the same sense of rhythm that goes with being able to evaluate a performance, or knowing when to cut or edit.

It always takes longer to get started than you hope. You always get more done in the second half of the day. Because the first half is often disappointingly slow, it's essential to have a minimum goal: a certain number of scenes covered before the lunch break. Or, in a studio where you're setting and lighting on the same day, perhaps to have begun recording at least something straightforward before the break. It's much easier to go on if you feel that you've actually achieved something already.

Keep it together

Just as the overall production schedule will already have grouped resources and places together as far as possible – so that all the filming in any given location happens consecutively – so you'll avoid too much movement backwards and forwards within the day, too.

It's obviously best to finish everything in the same room before moving on; but even within the same set-up, consider how much re-lighting is necessary to change angles, and organize the work to minimize the need to move lights backwards and forwards. Moving a lamp and then putting it back again might take only five minutes, but if you do it a dozen times during the day, that's an hour of your precious time when – possibly – you could have been doing something more productive.

On the other hand, it can be unsettling on performances if, in a drama, you do several different scenes from the same angle and then repeat them all from different angles. Sometimes it works, sometimes it can break the flow. It all depends on the cast and director. In the end you have to do what's best for the performance. That's what everyone is there for.

Even if you're only going to the room next door with a simple lighting set-up, it's likely to take around half an hour before you're ready to go again. Possibly it won't take as long, but realistically you should plan for it and remember to build that into the day's schedule. The transfer time can be speeded up by sending the gaffer along to pre-light it.

To do that, you need to have enough lamps – and whether the production can afford them is an earlier decision. The lighting cameraperson also needs to have seen the room and made a rough decision on how it's going to be lit. For this and other reasons it's a good idea to talk through the whole day with the cast and crew before you start. That way everyone knows what to expect – and how long the day is going to go on. And it means that everyone can think ahead to save time in moving from one location or scene to the next.

Enough is enough

Let's be honest, a director's position can be a lonely one. You are the person who has to decide whether and when something is good enough to accept, and you have to continually tread the line between perfection and the demands of the budget and the schedule.

There's often a temptation to do 'just one more' take, or set-up. Or 'This one's for Lloyd's' – an insurance shot. Just because, be honest, you're not confident enough that you have what you need.

If you've taken the time for proper homework before the shoot, you'll know how you intend to cover a scene, and you'll be able to adjust your plans in line with actual events without any trouble, because you know what the scene needs to achieve, and how you're going to cut it together.

So when you have what you need, and you have a good performance, then stop. Don't do any more. Go on to the next thing. By all means give yourself some cover, so that you have more than one way to cut it; but if you're not planning to use shots from 25 different angles, then don't waste time shooting them 'just in case'. In this kind of programme-making you haven't got the time.

People and performances

Landscapes, seascapes, wild-life, motor racing. There are other exceptions; but generally speaking practically all programme-making involves performances given by people. 'Performance' can mean a quick *vox pop* in the street, an interview with a politician, the participants in a game-show, or the most involving drama. In every case the camera is there solely to carry that performance to the viewers. You can dress it up with music and tricksy angles and cutting, or you can watch quietly; in the end it's still the performance that counts, and the performance that is the programme's reason for being.

Casting is crucial. Choose the right people and your work is half done, whether you're looking for a professional actor, or an interviewee. *Airport*, possibly the most successful of the docu-soaps was carried in the end by the personality of Jeremy, the man from Aeroflot. Fred Dibnah, a steeplejack, who appeared in one programme in the 1970s, later had several series devoted entirely to him.

Your job as director is to get the best out of the people in front of the camera as well as the people behind the camera. In fact, if you have the right people behind the camera, you should be able to concentrate on your cast or interviewees, or 'real people' and forget at that moment what the camera is doing, because you know that the camera is doing what you need it to do.

That remains true for every programme in every genre, however large the budget is. (Remember *The Phantom Menace,* where the actors seem to have been left to get on with it on their own?) And, whatever your budget is, when you're dealing with non-professionals – with real people – you can't keep repeating something until you get what you think you want. The contributors have to be comfortable enough to give a good performance the first time – and you have to be confident enough to know when you have it. Because it isn't going to get better as you hammer on.

The trick is to create a kind of bubble of calm around the performance. *You* know that the clock is ticking away and the meter running, and you have ten more of these to do today, but if you let your apprehension and impatience show, then you're lost. You'll never get what you need.

There are minor exceptions. At least one very well known television presenter is absolutely brilliant at learning a whole page of text to deliver to camera – providing that you do it straight away, and in no more than two takes. After that, it's gone. It can take all afternoon to get all the little bits you need to put it together afterwards, and it makes a nightmare of the editing.

Even if the task is simply to film people going about their daily business in a public place – a shopping centre, high street, restaurant – the way in which your crew handle themselves will influence the results you get. If you make a nuisance of yourselves and behave as if you own the place, people will react accordingly. You might even find the place suddenly empty. If you learn somehow to be unobtrusive, you will get what you need.

Being unobtrusive is a difficult trick for even a small crew, but it's interesting how quickly people forget that you're there if you just settle down, wait, and don't make a fuss. Fifteen minutes after you've arrived you really can be the fly on the wall. Once people see that you're not actually terribly interesting, they quickly get bored and go back to whatever it was they were doing before you arrived.

Most of this applies whatever your budget, but it's particularly important that you become skilled in relaxing and motivating people quickly, without hustling them, if you have a tight schedule to stick to.

Incidentally, the importance of the way you behave has repercussions beyond your particular programme. There was a time when visits from television crews were rare and fabulous events. Now most people have at least watched a crew at work, if not been involved with the making of a programme. The people who help you in your programme are doing just that. They are helping you. It has happened before and will happen again, that some crews seem to have a talent for travelling through the world closing doors behind them for any crew that follows, because they were so badly behaved. Don't be like that. You might need to go back. You might need to go where someone else has already been, and you can do without having to waste time convincing people that you will be different.

A director of my acquaintance was once involved in a day's filming with the help of the police to control traffic for the unit. They were friendly to the police, and the filming went well. Perhaps a year later, the same director was working in the country a few miles away, when a tractor started ploughing the field next to the camera. Clearly the farm-worker was hoping for a pay-off of some sort to stop ploughing. But then a police car drew up; the friendly policeman from the year before got out, told the farm-worker to go away, shook my colleague's hand, and drove off again. It pays to be friendly. You never know . . .

So keep your promises – including sending tapes of the programme afterwards; don't behave as if you own the place; don't leave it in a mess; put back all the furniture you moved. Own up and pay if you damage anything.

These are general rules, not just applicable to low-cost pro-gramme making; but, especially if you have no resources of time or money to spare, having to cope with the aftermath of someone else's bad behaviour can make toilet paper of your schedule – and therefore, your budget.

Interviews

Everyone develops their own way of doing interviews. However you conduct the interview *listen to the answers*. Obvious? You would have thought so, but on and off screen again and again you can see examples of interviewers who ask a question, and then bury themselves in their notes looking for the next question and let the interviewee get on with it all alone. Interviews are supposed to imitate the conventions of conversation.

One-sided conversations inevitably end up being statements – or trailing away altogether. It's not a good way to treat the people who are helping you, and, more important, you miss out on the follow-up questions that bring the prepared line of questioning to life.

It's also very hard to know if you have a good performance, or whether your interviewee has told the wonderful story you heard during the research conversations, if you're not listening to what's being said. If you have a list of questions, memorize it. Look at it at the end to make sure you've missed nothing. You will know from your research roughly the results you expect from the interview. Sometimes it's necessary to keep re-phrasing the question until your interviewee finally says what you know they've said before. Sometimes you really do have to say 'You told me this before, please can you say it again.' But it's always more natural and more convincing if you don't have to do that.

If an interview is live, or as-live, then of course the programme takes the whole interview and that's the end of it. Interviews conducted for later editing can either be constructed in a similar way, so that the answers can be dropped in to the final programme almost unedited, or a conversation can continue for much longer, in the knowledge that only a couple of minutes or so will be needed from a 20 or 30 minute interview.

The course of the interview needs to be closely steered in either case to ensure that the interview gives you what you need. Extra visual footage might need to be filmed as a result of something said during the interview. You need to listen with editing in mind. Some people talk in the way that Mahler writes music. Just when you think an end is coming, you're off on a new theme leading somewhere else entirely. It can make life difficult in the cutting room later.

Conventionally, an interview shoot will involve not only the interview itself, but cutaway questions (and reaction shots – noddies) from the interviewer, and perhaps mute two-shots which can be theoretically dropped in to conceal edits. If you don't shoot all of this (and many people don't) you must still be aware that you are going to need some cutaway material – ideally footage of whatever the interview is about, if that is practical. Make the decision before the shoot and keep the editor happy.

Efficient shooting is always aware of the edit.

Professionals

Professional performers – actors, presenters, and so on – should need less coaxing to a good performance than 'real people'; but everyone appreciates help in ensuring that the work they are doing is what the programme needs. And you, as the director, need to be sure that your talent is working on the same show as everyone else.

Actors are human, too. For whatever reason, some directors seem to display very short tempers, and sometimes wish to exercise an impractical degree of control over the people appearing in front of camera. In a nutshell, if you shout at people, and make them go for take after take, you are not going to get the best performance out of them.

Everyone has problems – sometimes inexplicable problems from time to time. I know an actor who had to count to ten in a scene. He got as far as six and couldn't for the life of him remember what came next. It's a kind of panic, but you don't fix it by shouting.

I'd say that if you haven't got the performance you need by take five or six, then it isn't going to get better. Either accept one of the takes you have, or go on to something else and come back to the troublesome scene later on. Nervous and tired people can't give their best. Professional technique can often disguise that fact from you and the audience, but it doesn't make it less true.

On *The Chef's Apprentice* there were two directors. One of them, an otherwise charming man, used to shout at actors, go up to take 56 on occasions, and routinely work until late in the evening. The other didn't. You can't tell from the finished programmes which was which, but the cast and crew certainly preferred finishing at 6 p.m. to finishing at midnight.

There are people who are taken more than somewhat with the glamour of the film and television industry. These people don't believe that real work is being done unless a shoot or an edit goes on all night. Don't believe it. Nobody works efficiently at 3 a.m. – especially if they've been there since eight the previous morning. Most people in our business are very hard workers. But people work best when they are not exhausted and – yes, dare to say it – when they are enjoying themselves. It's inefficient to drive people into the ground.

Three short days are likely to achieve much more than two very long ones – and probably cost less, too – unless the production is exploiting its team-members by not paying any overtime, of course.

Extended scenes

Some directors like to produce a performance in the cutting room. Taken to extremes, what the artist does is almost unimportant. Scenes are filmed from lots of different angles, often only a line or a couple of words at a time. The performance is constructed later from many short takes.

It's a perfectly valid way of working, but it isn't the most efficient way. Which makes it sound as if everything must be sacrificed to the god of efficiency. That certainly must not happen. But some working methods are better suited than others to making high quality programming on limited resources.

It is, I admit, a personal preference, but working in long takes gives the actors – or other performers – a better chance of contributing fully to the production if they are given a chance to get going and develop a rhythm of performance. It makes life easier for them because they don't have to keep stopping and remembering where they are in the scene. It makes life easier for the director and the crew because a performance is being staged, and all they have to do is follow it in the most appropriate way. To tell the story in the best way.

Naturally it will need several takes, and several different camera and lighting set-ups, to cover a scene. But if the scene is played through, then it's even possible to acquire more than one shot each time. One skill you have a right to expect from professionals is that they will do the same thing at the same point in the scene every time. The coffee-cup is always slammed on the table as they say 'What?!', so that you can cut between shots on the action if you decide to. (Actually the sound recordist wouldn't like it if the word and the cup going down were simultaneous, but you understand the idea.)

Certainly, it takes longer to rehearse a whole scene than a single line. But the chances of achieving a truly cohesive performance are much higher – and you're able to get through filming the whole scene more quickly in the end.

Real life

The director's task is to channel the differing preoccupations, skills, and desires to do well of everyone on the unit into making the same movie – the one that the director has already seen inside his or her head. The job is to turn this dream into reality.

Imagine this: the first day of a two-week shoot on a documentary series about witchcraft. You're about to interview the witch-queen of all England (or so she says). Traffic is abominable, so everyone arrives slightly late. The producer is keen to get going.

No, the crew can't have a break for coffee and a bacon roll, even though they've been driving for three hours.

The director points out that they can't do much until you've had a look at the room again and decided exactly where to put the camera. On the way upstairs (isn't it always on the top floor?) the cameraman is moaning about carrying all the so-called light-weight gear up the stairs.

How is everyone going to fit into this tiny room? Well, not everyone has to. The producer could wait outside when filming starts for one thing. And the producer can be useful now and chat to the nervous interviewee, while the crew bring the gear in. It's going to be half an hour before they're ready to go anyway.

The cameraperson decides that the only place the lights can go is in those corners, so the camera has to go there. But the director not only wants to use the window as a background, but wants to see the view, too. Luckily it's not a sunny day, but it still means more light on the inside to balance the exposure.

Will the ancient electrical circuits in the house melt under the strain of 2 kW lamps, each needing 8 amps? Will the interviewee melt under the heat?

So the cameraperson suggests a compromise: use the daylight as a key light and sit the person so that the window is not behind, but to one side. You can still see through it, but you're using the daylight rather than fighting it.

Sit the interviewee in the big chair, so, and give her a big book of spells as a prop. Does the background say something useful? OK we'll move things a little – 'Is that OK, your majesty?' – so that it does.

Time to get it lit, then. The spark puts down his copy of Proust and the bacon sandwich he has somehow acquired, and begins telling you of the time he worked on *Lawrence of Arabia*, at the same time complaining about the lack of power sockets in the house and the narrowness of the stairs.

The PA is asked to make her phone calls confirming the next location while sitting in the interviewee's chair as a lighting stand-in. And the sound recordist becomes increasingly dismayed as he sees his options for places to put not just his boom, but himself, slowly disappearing.

'You can sit on the floor in front of the camera', he is told.

Just then a road-drill starts up outside, and the recordist smiles glumly. 'I told you so.' The PA is sent to the producer to get a ten pound note to help persuade the road workers that its time to have a tea break. Not yet, when we say.

Finally everything appears to be ready. 'Just a couple more minutes' says the cameraman. After ten minutes of tweaks and moving the lamps an inch this way and back, and sending the spark to get another lamp and some more trace from the van – which is three streets away – the director has had enough. Time to start.

'Sure', says the cameraman, 'I was just playing around until you were ready.'

The interview goes well. The witch queen performs beautifully. The director asks the questions. The producer listens, and suggests one or two extra questions at the end. It all seems to be over, but the director needs some cutaways. Endless closeups of witchly artefacts and pages of books. The producer becomes restless. They are already late for their next appointment. 'Do you want a film or don't you?' asks the director, then finally calls a wrap.

The gear is all taken down and put on its boxes. Then the director has a thought – one more shot. He says. No, says the producer, and shuts the front door behind them.

And so it goes on, everyone with their own concerns, but somehow all working together – so that often a crew whose members have never met before, are asked at lunch time by the visiting client or commissioning editor whether they always work together.

Summary

❑ Keep looking at the schedule constantly during the day, and revising it if necessary. You will always have shots that would be nice, but may not be necessary. You can drop them.

❑ Always concentrate on the performance in front of the camera. Don't become so obsessed with the technology that you forget about the people, whether they are actors, presenters, or interviewees.

❑ Consider filming in long takes to give people a chance to develop a performance – again, whether they are actors or interviewees.

❑ In interviews – listen to the answers.

CHAPTER 10

CAMERAS – MAKING IT LOOK GOOD

Low budget productions are always pushed for time. If the truth be known, all productions are always pushed for time. Parkinson's law applies here, too. Activity expands to fill the time and money available. Still, low budget productions do have a particular problem.

However, it takes no more time to do something well, than to do it badly. There are always ways in which something could be done if more money or time were available. The trick is to think it through so that you do it well with the resources you do have available to you, rather than not well enough because you didn't have the resources you really wanted.

There are a number of ways in which a production can appear much glossier than the budget really allows – and this business is all about appearance in the end.

There's nothing wrong with production on hand-held DV cameras, using available light, if that is the look you want. It can be very immediate, giving a feeling of reality unrivalled by more traditional forms of production. It looks raw and real and wobbly. But it's important to do it on purpose rather than because you haven't worked out any other way. It's also possible with a few simple enough habits, to make your series look at least twice as expensive as it really was.

Where does the camera go? There are two stages to answering that question. The first stage involves the location. Visually interesting places look more expensive than bland ones. If you have to work in an office building rather than a stately home, at least choose an interesting part of it – with something going on in the background, for example.

The second stage involves where you put the tripod. Think about it, and then think again. Consider all 360 available degrees horizontally, and all possible vertical positions from floor to ceiling. Then decide. Don't just go for the 'obvious' option. Sometimes it may be the best. Often it's just a lazy choice.

The camera

Firstly, use a decent camera. Small cheap cameras are hard to move steadily, whether or not they are on a tripod. And the big give-away – the so-called 'DV look' – is that the cheaper chips and lenses can't hold down the highlights. Start looking, and you'll see unwanted flares, and burnt-out highlights everywhere in material shot on cheap DV cameras.

If you must use a consumer camera, then keep the contrast ratio low. And don't believe it when they say they can produce good pictures by candlelight, or in the cellar. Certainly, they can produce images, but the pictures will be noisy and the highlights will be burnt out. At least use a three-chip camera.

Give the camera a thorough test before you use it to see which automatic features work better than manual, and which ones don't. Automatic focus and exposure can be a boon in a difficult situation – the kind of shooting where these cameras are good – but can be a real problem in more controlled situations. You don't want the exposure opening up suddenly and the focus wallowing around just because someone has walked in front of the camera.

Lighting

Cameras have been able to achieve astonishing results under very low light levels for some time now. It's expected. There are two dangers here. The most obvious one is that the system (whether tape or film) is working very hard to produce an exposure at these low levels. The results will be noisy or grainy. Fine if that's what you want, but to be avoided otherwise.

Generally, however, you don't need lighting in order to raise the level of illumination, but quite simply, to make things look pretty. And making things look good can be done quite easily, and is one of the best ways to make the production look glossy.

The television screen is small. Movie buffs have always complained (quite rightly) that the big screen has an impact that television can't match. But, although the television screen can't give you the Cinemascope experience, one thing it does have is

Figure 10.1 Shots with depth: El Espejo, Madrid.

depth. Because all the viewer's attention is focused on a fairly small area, it's not hard to give the illusion that the world inside the box extends back for a great distance.

How do you do it? Avoid putting people in corners. The script calls for a dialogue across a kitchen table between two characters: move the table as far as possible from the wall, and put a streak of light across the background; or shoot towards the window, if possible balancing the light inside to match the exterior so that you can actually see through the window.

The programme needs an interview with a company's chief executive. If they can't be persuaded out of their office, move them away from the wall to create some depth behind them. Or switch on the desk light, close the blinds, and use only the desk light. Do almost anything to avoid a bland, grey or brown suit sitting in a bland grey or brown office.

The standard lighting kit tends to consist of a mixture of Redheads (800W) and Blondes (2000W). Very often you don't need anything like this much light. It's hard to control. It heats the room and makes everyone uncomfortable. Much more interesting results can be achieved with a number of small lamps, such as a set of 12V Dedo lights, or smaller conventional lamps such as Pups or Mizars.

Planes

It is very often possible to create three or four different layers of depth in a picture. For example: the subject in the foreground, a table just behind, a plant on a window sill behind that, and then the view out of the window.

If the camera then moves (if it's appropriate), the layers will move relative to each other, as well. It's just more interesting than a simple talking head stuck in a corner. Though, of course, whatever you do must add to, rather than detract from, what is being said.

Figure 10.2 Shots with depth: Café Sperl, Vienna.

Reflectors

The problem with shooting against the light is that the background is lit and the foreground is not. Simply using a reflector can make a surprisingly big difference to the look of a shot. Most camera kits that you'll hire (or that your cameraperson puts together) have some sort of a reflector, but even a sheet of white paper can help – for example to reduce the depth of the shadow in areas of bright sunlight.

I've recently seen a programme which featured interior shots in a cinema foyer. The sequence was filmed on DV by available light, and the presenter was standing in front of an illuminated poster with the result that the poster was perfectly exposed and the presenter's face was in darkness. A reflector to gather the available light and put it on the presenter's face would have made an enormous difference. As it was, the shot was not only not funky, it was irritating.

Battery lights

A sun gun can be very useful in strong daylight to fill shadows, or combined with a reflector to diffuse their harshness in low light conditions. But unless you want that 'good enough for news' look, you should try not to use them direct – especially not on the camera axis. And lights on top of the camera always look amateurish. Fine if you want that look, but it looks like a quick and rough news report, not like a feature film.

Tripods and dollies

Always use a tripod. Some of my personal favourites use handheld cameras – *Hill Street Blues, The Bill, The Renford Rejects* – quite apart from all the conventions led by MTV. However, I believe very strongly that the decision to take the camera off the tripod must be a deliberate one. Although hand-held cameras can produce a powerful sense of reality and involvement for the audience, they can also look sloppy and lazy. Over-wild movement is interesting and exciting when it's relevant to the subject. But it can also alienate, and betray a lack of confidence in the subject – a fear that without hysterical camera movement, nobody is going to stick with the programme because it's otherwise too boring.

Camera, graphic and editing style should *always* develop from the subject and nature of the programme. Otherwise all you have is a collection of pretty but vacant boxes.

Nothing exudes a feeling of quality as much as a tracking shot (or a similar Steadicam move). There are several tracking systems based on plastic piping and a box with wheels on which the tripod stands. Very Heath Robinson, but they work very well under the right circumstances. You have to be working on a fairly flat surface, because one thing you can't do with this sort of equipment is to wedge the track up to level it, which is what you often do with the much more expensive Elemack. They work very well on paved surfaces and indoors – and at maybe £70 a day most productions can afford them. A jib arm can also be added to give the camera some degree of vertical movement.

Steadicam is by no means a cheap alternative to a dolly and tracks – but there are also cheaper Steadicam clones for around £100 a day. They tend to be limited in the weight of camera they can carry, but may well be adequate for your shoot.

Of course, you need a good operator. The Steadicam operator's, or dolly grip's sense of timing will make an enormous difference to the quality of your shots. I remember being knocked out by a move on *The Chef's Apprentice.* The actor came out of the castle, mounted a horse, and rode away. The camera tracked maybe five metres, and craned up two metres at the same time to follow. The move was all so perfectly timed with the action that on the screen you were not really aware that the camera was moving at all. The art that conceals art.

The other major advantage of tracking shots is that they use up screen time. A choreographed, moving shot, is not one shot in editing terms, but several, since it changes all the time. It may take a little longer to set up and rehearse, but you get much more interesting screen time out of it. When you have a very tight schedule, you need to be able to make maximum use of everything you shoot.

Even if you are using a large number of tracking shots, it's sensible to cover yourself by shooting static versions of the same action to cut away to, and with which you can adjust the time the movement takes.

It's even more important to cover yourself if your camera is not moving. Once a scene is established, you need something else to cut to. You can't usually use another wide shot, but you can use any number of close-ups. Just make sure that you have them available.

Particularly in a documentary situation you can never shoot enough close-ups. Always get as many as time permits; because you will later discover that you haven't got as many of those usable moments as you thought at the time. But don't shoot material just for the sake of it. You should always be aware of where you might use a shot. If you can't use it, don't shoot it. It's just a waste of time, both at the shoot, and in the edit.

Wide-screen

Increasingly, wide-screen production is being expected in the UK, in any case. But there's no doubt that something produced in wide-screen always looks glossier than its 4:3 equivalent. However, wide-screen television is not widespread in the world. Even within the UK, the camera operator and the director need to be aware of three different levels of picture cut-off.

A wide-screen production wants to use the full available width of the 16:9 ratio. And so it should. Except that it mustn't, because not everyone has wide-screen television sets, and some people don't like watching programmes in letterbox format, so producers are expected to ensure that the 4:3 area of the wide-screen picture is 'protected', that is, that the picture makes sense if all you can see is an area of it in a ratio of 4:3. That area will be the central part of the picture, so short of spending ages in post production producing a special 4:3 version of the programme the production has to make sure that all the important action happens in the middle of the screen. Which is a bit of a waste of the wide-screen format.

To further complicate the whole affair, some broadcasters transmit in a compromise 14:9 format, which is still wide-screen, but reduces the size of the black bands of the top and bottom of the screen.

If the production is directly commissioned by a broadcaster who will transmit in wide-screen, there's not much of a problem. You produce 16:9, or whatever you agree with the broadcaster. If, however, you (or they) intend to sell the programmes overseas, you'll have to try to fit in with the requirement to protect the 4:3 area, and possibly the 14:9 area as well. As someone said of the computer industry, 'We love standards. That's why we have so many of them.'

Increasingly, cameras are switchable between 4:3 and 16:9 formats. On cheaper cameras, it may be better to ignore the switch and to mask a 16:9 area in post-production, to ensure that you're making maximum use of the pixels available on the camera's chip.

Summary

Hand-held DV shooting is a perfectly good style for the right subject. But it's only a style. Otherwise:

❏ Always use a tripod.
❏ Tracking or Steadicam shots look classy and use up screentime.

❏ You can never have too many close-up or mid-shot cutaways, but you can only establish a scene once.

❏ Take advantage of the depth of the television screen. Light for depth.

❏ Lighting isn't for illumination, it's for making things look good.

❏ Produce everything wide-screen, but be very careful of the 4:3 protected area.

CHAPTER 11

MICROPHONES – MAKING IT SOUND GOOD

As any sound recordist will tell you, sound is massively under-appreciated in film and television. Everyone concerns themselves with getting the pictures – 'This is, after all, a visual medium', they say – and the recordist is ignored at best, and moaned at for getting in the way – or, worse, for asking for another take when the pictures were perfect.

That's the way of the world, I'm afraid. Sound is one of those things that people don't notice unless it goes wrong, and the skills of the sound recordist and the boomswinger are unlikely ever to be fully appreciated.

Consider this, however: much of factual and documentary television is dominated by interviews in various forms. Nothing wrong with that. Now, imagine you've been out on the road and filmed a number of interviews. Everything has gone very well, until you find that there's a technical problem with the material. Which is worse – to have no pictures, or to have no sound? I'd say that if you have good sound you can always find pictures from somewhere to cover it. If you have a talking head and no sound, what can you use it for?

There's competent sound, and there's good sound. Taking a little bit more care and not simply taking the easiest option can make a big difference to the feeling of quality that a production has.

Stereo

First of all, make every programme in stereo. Remember the last time you went and sat in the dark in the movies – that big, wide sound? Even on television, the sound can have something of that effect – particularly for those viewers who feed their television sound through their hi-fi or home cinema systems – which is increasingly likely, particularly amongst viewers of satellite channels.

In the real world, of course, although you can record interview sound in stereo, there isn't much point, since it's basically a mono sound source, which you can later place anywhere you like in the stereo 'picture'. Yes, you can tell the difference, but most people can't.

Something that will make the difference is stereo effects. By all means record the interview in mono, but record the atmosphere track in stereo. (You do always record an atmos track at every location, don't you?) It's amazing how much difference that can make to the depth of the sound, even with a mono interview in the foreground. The atmos track can be recorded on a separate DAT machine. In fact having a DAT recorder on which to record effects has the additional benefit that the camera isn't tied up recording sound. The recordist can go and do something useful while the scene is being lit and do the crossword later.

Music, of course, should always be recorded and mixed in stereo, and in practice, most programmes have stereo music and effects, but the dialogue and interviews are recorded in mono and put in the right place on the sound stage during the mix. Studio-based shows are obviously different in this respect, since if you don't get it at the time, you can't do too much to it later.

Radio microphones, or 'I'm looking for a boom shadow'

Radio microphones are the greatest thing since sliced bread; or quite simply a curse.

When radio-mics are good

In music production, where the microphone has to be as close as possible to the performer's mouth in order for the sound mixer to be able to control the balance of voice and instruments, radio microphones, whether on a headset, taped to the cheek or hand-held, are absolute magic, completely solving all the problems of ugly, unwieldy trailing cables. In a wide shot in drama or documentary productions where the performers are necessarily a long way from the camera, radio microphones make sync shots possible where they otherwise wouldn't be. And in shows where presenter or performers have to move around a great deal, radio microphones are essential.

But, at the same time, radio lapel microphones (personal microphones, if you prefer) are a curse. They are very often used lazily and sloppily, and produce a truly terrible sound: muffled, too close, quite often breaking up because of some cable or transmission fault. If you don't believe me, try listening to interviews and discussions where you can see that this sort of microphone is being used. Even on the loudspeaker of your TV at home, they usually sound terrible.

Of course lapel microphones can be essential under certain circumstances. But a similar rule should be applied here as to tripods. Don't use them unless the decision is consciously made. If a production is to sound glossy, under control, and well put together, then it should use boom microphones wherever possible. This may require an extra crew member to put the microphone in the right place, but sound is important. It's a decision that needs to be taken seriously. Don't go on a documentary shoot with your sound kit and use the lapel mics for everything, and the gun-mic only for atmos.

And never use the camera-mic, unless the only alternative is a mute shot.

Cameramen like radio lapel mics because it means there's no possibility of having to move their lights to give the boom-swinger somewhere to go where they can work without casting a boom shadow. Sound recordists prefer them because it makes their life easier. But they don't produce good sound.

One thing small personal mics are excellent for is getting sound in small aircraft. Rather than plugging film equipment into the aircraft intercom directly, a small microphone fits easily inside the earpiece of the passenger's headset, and will pick up conversation inside the aircraft as well as everything on the radio from air traffic and other aircraft.

Perspective

One of the biggest problems with sound from lapel mics is that the sound perspective is fine in close-ups, but move the camera back to a wider shot, and you expect the sound to open out, too. Lapel mics give you the same close-miked sound whatever you do, and it can be disturbing. I once filmed a dream sequence using personal microphones – it was perfect for that strange 'voices-in-your-head' feeling that you get in dreams, because the sound perspective was wrong.

A boom hovering on the edge of frame automatically gives you the right sound perspective, because whenever the camera moves back, the microphone has to go with it. But it does lead to problems when the picture becomes too wide. Although by then the picture is probably too wide to see lip-sync, and the dialogue can be re-recorded later.

Also, when one actor is closer to the camera than the other, the boom balances the perspective automatically.

Having the microphone too far away is actually more of a problem, because it makes everything sound as if it were recorded in a bathroom. Using camera-mics *always* gives you this effect. However good-looking the pictures, the reverberant sound says only one thing to the viewer: 'art-film' if they're being kind, 'amateur film' if they're not.

Summary

❑ Produce as much as possible in stereo.
❑ At least be sure to shoot stereo sound effects and atmosphere tracks wherever you go.
❑ Avoid lapel mics as far as possible. Use a boom or a gun-mike to get high-quality open sound with the right perspective for the picture.
❑ Never use the camera mic unless the shot would otherwise be mute.
❑ Get the highest quality sound you can at the time of shooting. You can always degrade it later, but you can't put back what was never there.

POST-PRODUCTION

Do you need it?

Once upon a time all television was live, then videotape came along, and gradually it became the habit to record nearly everything. With a few rare exceptions, only news programmes, sport, some daytime magazine programmes, and links are broadcast live these days. Even supposedly live chat shows are usually recorded an hour or two in advance, so that any uncomfortable intrusions of real life can be removed to protect the audience.

But there's no reason why certain types of programme should not be treated as if they were live, and recorded as such. You may remember that we did our food programme in that manner, coming out at the end of the day with two programmes of precisely the right length.

There's never any absolutely good or bad way of solving the problem of how best to use the resources of time and money you have available, but this is certainly one way of saving on post-production costs – don't do any post-production.

Preparation

It's the same in every stage of programme-making. Paper is cheap. The more clearly thought-out each process is before the production begins to spend money on expensive equipment and people, the more smoothly and efficiently the process is likely to be conducted. This is actually the opposite of being inflexible. If the programme has a solid structure, then it allows proper time and consideration to be given to adding that extra detail and flair that turn a competent programme into an outstanding one. If the editing budget and schedule are entirely consumed in establishing a workable structure for the programme, then there won't be time for any frills, and the result is something which looks like a cheap programme.

A few years ago I was involved in making a number of corporate and training productions. Very often the typical schedule for a 12–15 minute programme would be something like:

Thursday: meet the client and be briefed
Friday: write the script
Monday: script changes and set up the shoot
Tuesday, Wednesday: filming
Thursday: commentary recording and paper edit
Friday: on-line edit and programme delivery.

I couldn't honestly recommend that as an ideal schedule, and it wasn't always like that, but it was certainly a very educational time – and, luckily, there were no real disasters.

There are three stages to making the edit work in a situation like this.

The first one is to have a script which makes sense, even though you don't necessarily know everything that will happen during the filming. However you do it, you are ultimately telling a story, even if you do it in the most impressionistic way. Don't lose sight of the story.

Second, with the script and programme structure in mind, continually go through your shopping list of the footage you need; take advantage of anything unexpected that arises during filming; but don't film it if you don't know what you're going to do with it.

Third, with a good shot-list and your memory of the shoot, go through the script and write in the shots, with timecode numbers, in the places you think you'll use them: the paper edit.

As I say, I wouldn't advocate that kind of schedule as a production habit; and technology has moved on to give video editing all the flexibility of film, with auto-conforming that really works; but the habits which make that sort of production possible are useful in any kind of production.

The editor

The editor has a massive influence over the quality of the final programme. There are basically two main kinds of editor: those who come from an engineering, or on-line editing background; and those who come from a film editing, or off-line editing background.

In an on-line edit there is very little opportunity to do more than tidy up the programme as defined in the edit decision list – and that's as it should be. Editors who gain their experience in this kind of environment – particularly if it's inside a broadcasting organization – are used to doing what they're told by the director. Their skill and experience often makes them able to do wonderful things instantly, with the millions of buttons they have available, but what they are not practised at doing is beginning with the rushes and making a programme out of it with only minimal input from a director.

On the other hand, the tradition in film – whether feature films or television – is that the editor has a large degree of autonomy. The editor's contribution to the programme is as great as that of the cinematographer, and they should be treated at the same level, as a skilled craftsman or woman with a high degree of responsibility.

The skill here is not as obvious as that of the pilots of the Starship Enterprise on-line suites. After all, it doesn't take long to learn how to chop a piece of film in a joiner, or drag a file from the bin on one part of the screen to the timeline at the bottom. But, as with most other things in programme-making, it's certainly not difficult to learn which button to press. It's learning when to press it that takes the rest of your life.

Directors also tend to be divided in the way they work in post-production. Some feel that they need to be in the cutting room all day every day. Others are content to give the editor overall instruction and guidance, and leave them to do their bit of the job on their own. There's no right way to do it, and different combinations of director and editor will work out their own preferred methods.

In a sentence, the editor's art resides in a strong sense of rhythm. Given that a programme is put together with the right pictures in the right order to tell the story effectively (something which in itself is by no means simple), the pace and timing of the cutting makes all the difference between a programme which draws the viewer in and along with it, and one which plods along, stopping and starting and losing interest – and viewers – as it goes.

This difference of feel can be created by decisions about where to cut shots between one frame and the next – that is, a difference of $\frac{1}{25}$ of a second (in PAL) can make certain cuts flow ... or crunch. Certainly two frames – $\frac{1}{12}$ of a second – can make an enormous difference.

Video-based production has brought the ultimate safety net: if the programme doesn't work out because of the way it's edited, you can always junk the edit you don't like and start again. But you don't really want to do that.

Cost-efficient programme-making recognizes the skills of the good editor, and finds an editor who is not only good, but also able to work quickly.

Procedures

At the simple extreme, a production that was recorded multi-camera in long scenes, or as live, doesn't need much editing. All that remains to be done in post-production is a little tidying up, or possibly stringing scenes together in script order. In this case there isn't usually much point in going through an off-line stage at all. It would cost time and effort without saving anything very much in the on-line suite. The edit still needs to be properly prepared, even if there isn't much to do. On-line edit suites are never cheap.

By contrast, a programme filmed in several countries, involving lots of extended interviews, will be a nightmare to edit unless you take an organized approach. The off-line edit process is considerably less costly than filming, but it is also considerably more expensive than time spent in preparation on paper.

Proper thought is just as important at the post-production stage as at any time before. Too many productions stay within budget and schedule until the shoot finishes, and then throw it all away in the edit.

First of all, you don't want too much material. The more tapes you have from the shoot, the longer it's going to take to sort them out in the edit. The cost of the stock alone may not be enough to influence your shooting ratio, but you'll regret having a hundred tapes of rushes for a half hour programme.

Cutting order

Before the director begins working with the editor – or before she or he begins cutting if they are doing it for themselves – it's essential to produce a cutting order. The cutting order need be nothing more than a marked-up script. If you've managed to keep hold of the story happily through the pre-production and the shoot – what's the story, how are we telling it? – then everything will fall happily into place.

If you need to look through all the rushes, then the time to roll backwards and forwards looking for shots is at home or in the office with VHS tapes, not in the edit suite. By the time you go there, you need to have a good idea of where everything is.

It may be that you feel you don't need to watch all the rushes. I have to say that I find viewing rushes very tedious. I know what I've shot, and the timecode logs are detailed enough for me to be able to find things easily when I need them; but that's just the way of working I happened to have developed.

Transcripts

If the programme involves anything but a few short interviews, it's absolutely essential to have transcripts made. It takes a very long time – and most of it is wasted – to run through interviews on either video or audio tape until you know them well enough to pick out the sound bites you need to tell the story. If there are lots of interviews, you also have to remember who said what. In a word, a complete nightmare. Don't do it.

Provide whoever is doing the transcripts with a VHS cassette with burnt-in timecode. The timecode should be noted on the transcript at least as often as each time a question is asked. It takes time to transcribe interviews. Tapes should be sent to the person doing transcripts as soon as possible – ideally at the end of the day on which the interview is filmed. That way most of them will be ready when filming is over.

The director can then go through the interviews relatively rapidly. Paper is, after all, a non-linear medium. You can read at any point and skip to any other point. Use the first reading for familiarization – to remind yourself of what was said, and put it in context with all the other interviews, because (except for the last one you filmed, of course) you won't have known what everyone else was going to say at the time you filmed the interview. Read through all the interviews before you go on.

During the second reading, start lightly marking out interesting sentences and remarks. Don't try to be too precise yet, you probably don't know the material quite well enough. You'll only change your mind – or mark up too much.

Finally go through a third time, one interview at a time, and precisely mark out the sections you think you're going to use. Put a box round the exact words, so that the editor (and anyone else who needs to) is quite clear about what you've decided on. And give each of these boxes a unique code – an interview with Michael Caine could have codes MC1, MC2. It doesn't matter, as long as it makes sense to you and everyone else. There'll be more than you need. Several people might say similar things, and you'll have to decide later which to use. Give yourself a choice, but also be sure that the most important selection is made now. All of this can be done on paper. Occasionally an edit made on paper won't work on the screen, because the intonation is wrong at the end; or because what looks like a nicely completed sentence on paper turns out to have its words running into the beginning of the next sentence. Don't worry about it now. As long as choices are available, all that can be sorted out later.

It's tedious, but it saves a tremendous amount of trouble in the long run: all production paperwork should be clear – and you can never provide too much information, from call-sheets and schedules, through shoot logs, to marked up transcripts and music cue sheets. You may be able to remember it all now, but you won't still remember in two years time when you're asked who said something, or you have to make an alteration.

Whether the programme is commissioned by a broadcaster, or delivered to a distributor, part of the delivery process involves providing a completed 'Programme as Completed', or 'Programme as Broadcast' form, which contains details of all contributors, crew, music and archive film used – everything that went into the programme. It's a bore to do, but if proper notes and records are kept, it should involve no more than copying information from your paperwork to the form. If the production paperwork is not maintained properly, then it can take days to round up all the information you need.

To continue with the transcripts: each interview now has a selection of usable quotes marked-up and identified. Make a list of them interview by interview, with a bullet-point phrase or a sentence identifying each code. By now you'll know the material pretty well, and you'll have reduced its essentials to a list that's only one or two pages long. And it's much easier to keep track of a two-page list than of 200 pages of transcript.

Running order

Assuming the bullet-point phrases you've used are an adequate shorthand for the sections of interview you've selected, you can now use the bullet points to fit the interview bites into the structure of the programme.

The end result is a cutting order which might be rather strange looking, composed largely of codes like: MC3, GG6, MK15 – but it makes perfect sense.

If the marking up is then transferred to the transcript files on computer – by shading the chosen areas, for example – then the marked up transcript can be printed out as many times as necessary, saving the bother of photocopying. And a paper assembly can be made by cutting and pasting the WP files to match the cutting order you've just produced.

The editor needs the entire marked-up transcript, as well, of course, otherwise she or he won't know where the sound bites come from – but both are easily transported or e-mailed, so that isn't a problem.

Digitizing

Presuming that the edit process will be a computer-based non-linear off-line edit (Avid, Lightworks, and the like), while the director is going through transcripts, the editor can begin digitizing. There's no point in digitizing all the rushes. It uses up storage space on the system, and (more important, as hardware becomes cheaper, and systems have more storage available) it means that you still have masses of stuff to look through when making edit decisions.

Select what you know to be good takes of visual material. You can always digitize some more if you need it later. Don't digitize any interviews until you have marked-up transcripts ready; then digitize only the marked-up sections, and give them the same references as the codes in the transcript (MM24, or whatever).

Another reason for not digitizing more than you need is that the data that you do digitize will need to be backed up, because the editing computer will have another programme to do after yours. Probably it will be another programme in the same series. And there won't be enough storage for the first programme to stay on the computer. Backing up and restoring takes time, which can eat into schedules, even if the production is not charged for it.

Assembly

With this level of preparation, the first assembly of a half-hour programme should take no more than a half a day, at the end of which you'll have a programme which is too long, but which gives you a feeling for how it's going to work in the end.

Slash and burn

You can then go through the assembly transcript and make further cuts on paper, before carrying them out in the cutting room. It's much easier to see if the juxtaposition of two interview clips makes sense on paper in the first instance. It's also easier to make sure that whatever commentary you write fits in with what comes before and after if you can see it in front of you, rather than having to run the pictures again and again.

The editor still has plenty of work to do to refine the programme, and turn it into a good film; but this kind of method gets the structure sorted out early on. Once everyone involved in decision making is happy that the structure is working, everything else follows much more easily – and won't be wasted effort. The last thing you want to happen is that a programme is produced which is a beautiful piece of film-making, but where a commissioning editor, or producer decides that the story structure isn't working, so that the whole thing has to be all but totally recut.

The programme with lots of lengthy interviews certainly lies at the other extreme from simply tidying up a studio-based multi-camera show. But the principles of organization are the same wherever you are along the spectrum.

Go into the cutting room with a cutting order properly prepared. Quite likely the result won't be quite what you wanted, but at least you'll have something to change. Making changes to an edit – responding to what's already there – is much more efficient and rewarding than staring hopelessly at rushes hoping that the editor will somehow be able to make it all right for you. Worse if you're the editor as well.

Break things up

One of the first casualties of very low-budget programming is variety. There just isn't enough time to produce all the material that you would ideally like to. The programme has to make do with one or two locations, where more would have been preferable.

However, there's a lot you can still do. The essence of making a programme interesting and lively is to keep things changing. It may not be possible with your programme's resources to provide lots of completely different elements, but that doesn't mean that your only option is long pieces to camera, or lengthy two-shot interviews.

This is a particularly good example of the way in which it's important to consider the edit (the end of the programme-making process, if you like) right from the beginning. When resources are limited, it's vital to plan to make the best of them.

Perhaps the programme is constrained such that it has to contain the entire action in three locations. Construct the action so that, rather than telling the story in a completely linear fashion – section A takes place in location A, section B in location B, followed by section C in location C – mix it all up, so that you can cut ABABACBC, or some such. If you keep things changing, your audience won't notice that you didn't have the budget to travel the world. In the end it's the story and the way it's told that keeps audiences, not how many locations the series is able to take its camera to.

Cutting to length

Non-linear editing makes it easy to cut a programme to exactly the right length.

In the days of linear-only tape editing, there were two choices in adjusting the length of a programme edit. You could copy the whole programme (except the sections you no longer wanted) to another tape. This meant that you went down a generation, which is acceptable within limits, but something to be avoided where possible. Certainly it isn't something you should or could do repeatedly without noticing a significant loss of quality. If you make too many copies of copies of copies in film you can eventually see a phenomenon known as 'colour crossover' where the reds and greens (for instance) are reversed – strange effect.

Alternatively, if you wanted to avoid going down further generations in your programme, you had to re-edit the whole thing from the point where you made the first change.

The bad old days are gone from that point of view – although the problems of multiple generations are still with us, but further on in the post-production process. Non-linear editing means that shots can be moved around, trimmed, shuffled, extended, in video just as easily as they always could be on film.

The major problems in bringing in a programme to exactly the right length are no longer technical, they are conceptual. A first cut of a programme is invariably much too long. That's a good thing. It's a much bigger problem if you haven't enough material to fill the required time. If the first cut is twice as long as it should be that's forgivable. If it's any longer, the next stage will probably be harder than it need be.

However essential the dedicated programme-maker feels material to be to a true depiction of the subject, or a true telling of the story, in the end the programme has to fit the required running time, and material will have to be dropped.

Actually, a great many programmes (or series) still end up too long. Most programmes would benefit from being condensed still further, but there are vast amounts of airtime to fill, and programme schedulers like long series, because (a) they have a chance to build a loyal audience, which, obviously, a single programme cannot do, and (b) they can make one decision which takes care of their programming requirements for the next three or six months, and don't have to worry about what to do in that slot for a while.

Nibbling at the problem in the hope that you'll suddenly find the programme has come down to the right length is likely to be a long, painful, and ultimately unsuccessful process. There's no substitute for being bold. Cut whole sections. Then run the programme. The real test is not, 'Did you notice something missing?' because you always will, if you know it was there; but, 'Does someone who doesn't know the story feel the lack of information or explanation?'

It's surprising how much can go from the first cut, and still leave the story completely intact. More than that, very often the story is clearer and told more powerfully without the extraneous material. It's important to be aware enough to see that if this is the case.

Finally, in this context, one of the more important benefits of having an editor who was not present at the shoot is that she or he will be able to look at the material objectively. A shot or an interview or a performance is good if it works on the screen. It doesn't matter that you spent all day up to your neck in water getting it, nor that it took three years of careful persuasion to entice this person in front of the camera. If it doesn't work, drop it. Once the programme is finished and shown, nobody will know. What's on the screen is the only thing that matters.

Summary

❏ Post-production is the area which most often runs away with the budget. Don't relax after the shoot. Be organized.
❏ The more the editing process is one of refinement, the more painlessly it works. Make broad decisions at the beginning, then refine that material, then further refine what you have left, and so on until you've finished.
❏ Always produce a cutting order.
❏ Don't try to select interview clips by listening – do it on paper.
❏ Don't digitize everything; it wastes time and resources.

CHAPTER 13
DV AND DESKTOP EDITING

A very short time ago, really, non-linear editing was synonymous with two major companies: Avid (Mac-based) and Lightworks (PC-based). They led a revolution in production methods, and they were both very expensive, because the computer hardware was very expensive. Since then the cost of disk storage, fast processors, and memory has dropped like a stone and continues to do so. The office computer of today is quite powerful enough to edit video.

This has caused corporate problems amongst the pathfinder companies: Lightworks is no more; Avid is struggling to find a place for itself.

For the rest of us it's important to realize that the badge on the hardware is unimportant. As with any computer-based system, the question should be, 'What do I need to achieve? What software do I need to run?' Then buy the hardware to do the job properly. It's perfectly possible to construct your own on-line broadcast standard desktop edit suite for a fraction of the cost of the turnkey brand-name systems. This brings obvious advantages, but has several drawbacks.

How to do it

With apologies to fans of the Mac, PCs are still more flexible and better value for money.

The PC industry is lead by computer games. Apart from specialized workstations, which are in a quite different league as far as cost is concerned, the most powerful machines on the market are the fastest games machines, because computer gaming has always stretched the hardware to its limits – and beyond.

So the first step is to acquire a PC which has been designed to be a fast games performer. Don't go to a retailer. Ideally find a small company near to you that builds PCs to order. If they understand video editing, so much the better; the value of having someone you can talk to when problems occur cannot be underestimated; and if you do have hardware problems, or wish to up-grade later on, the fact that your supplier is geographically quite close can make life a great deal easier.

You need to have at least 128 Mb of system memory (RAM), and you cannot really have too much disk space.

The DV family has a standard compression ratio of 5:1 and has a standard data rate of 3.6 Mb per second. Video requires approximately 200 Mb of disk space per minute. Differences between mini DV and DVCAM, for example, are in the way the data is written to tape. The picture signal is the same.

A 25 minute programme uses 5 Gb of disk space. If, for the edit, you digitize (actually that's the wrong expression for DV, since the signal is already digital) five times as much material as the final programme needs, then you'll be using 25 Gb of disk space. In reality, you need more than that, because you'll need room for rendered effects, extra audio, and temporary and data files associated with the edit.

So, in the real world, your system should have at least 30 Gb of fast disk space available to it – in addition to the basic hard disk containing the operating system and program files.

The normal internal hard disk will be acceptable, but really the disk should be a fast SCSI drive, specially intended for audio-visual use (these are high quality drives designed not to interrupt data flows by the re-calibration processes that normal drives go through every few seconds).

Ideally, you should also have a back-up system that can handle that amount of data, although you could argue that it's only necessary to be able to re-digitize the video again.

Capture cards: analogue

How do the pictures get from videotape to your computer? There are two fundamental choices: analogue or digital.

The earlier capture cards were analogue, in that they converted a traditional composite or component video signal into (typically) motion JPEG (MJPEG) video files on the computer. Normally, the video output quality of these cards is similar to VHS. They are the basis of purely off-line systems. Edit decisions are made on the computer, and an edit decision list (EDL) and a viewing VHS tape are produced. The EDL is then taken to a traditional on-line edit suite and the edit automatically replicated using the original camera tapes to produce the broadcast master.

The advantage of this method is that capture cards are now available for very low prices – no longer £2500, but perhaps a tenth of that. The capabilities are the same. In fact, sometimes the cards are the same.

Also, the compression ratio on capturing video to MJPEG files is normally adjustable. Rather than requiring the 200 Mb of disk space per minute that DV footage needs, perfectly usable results can be produced (for viewing purposes) at ratios using only 50 Mb per minute or less. The same hard disk is suddenly four times the size!

Capture cards: digital

Capturing digital video (DV) is actually a data transfer from tape to your disk. Most DV cameras and VCRs have something which is variously called 'Firewire', 'i-Link', or a '1394' port. This is connected to a similar port on the capture card on the computer. Firewire (or IEEE1394) is a standard for moving large quantities of data at high speed. Firewire ports are standard on the Mac; the standard was originally invented by Apple as a high-speed general-purpose port. It was capable of such unnecessarily high speeds that no other manufacturer took it up until digital video came along – a classic case of a solution being too early for the problem.

Low-cost DV capture cards are in reality IEEE1394 interface cards with specialist drivers written to handle DV. All the work of processing the DV data, displaying it, and controlling the DV camcorder or VCR is done by these software drivers. Usually this means that full-screen video cannot be displayed on the computer monitor, but that the hardware CODEC (coder/ decoder) in the camcorder or VCR is used instead. The edit output is displayed on a normal television monitor attached to the video output of the camcorder or VCR.

The more expensive DV capture cards have hardware CODECs on the card, and are consequently able to display full-motion full-screen video on the computer monitor. They also tend to be smoother to work with, and quicker to render and display visual effects.

You get what you pay for. But cards incorporating hardware CODECs will become cheaper. In the meantime it is perfectly possible to edit without pain with the cheaper cards. Because you are simply copying a broadcast standard signal to your disk, selecting the bits you want, and then copying the result back to tape, this is effectively an on-line edit suite for the cost of a desktop computer and a capture card.

Of course this kind of system can't replace a full on-line edit suite. And of course the picture quality is limited by that of the DV system. It would be foolish to pretend that it was the equal of a full Digital Betacam or D9 system, for instance.

However, it's the DV format that counts. Digital Betacam or D9 camera equipment is not particularly expensive to hire. Odd though it might seem, material shot on Digi Beta, transferred to DV or DVCAM, and then edited on a desktop system, will give you results that are at least as good as those of a conventional Betacam SP edit. Better, because there will be no problem with dropouts.

I repeat, though, that I am not asserting that the results obtained from using a domestic DV camcorder for acquisition are to be seriously compared to top end cameras. The quality is astounding, considering the cost of the equipment, but that is as far as it goes.

Sound

How much you spend on the sound side of your system depends on how much work you intend to do on the programme sound, and how much you will be taking to an outside facility. The quality of sound from video is not affected by the quality of the sound card in your computer. If the system is designed for DV editing through the 1394 interface, the sound is part of the video data and doesn't go through the sound card on your system except for monitoring.

Some analogue capture cards capture audio as well as video, in which case the system sound card is not involved in input or output quality for analogue off-line editing either, but is still used for monitoring.

However, it is possible to perform an off-line edit and produce an EDL for the vision, but mix the sound 'on-line' on the computer. The mixed track is then played off to DAT or CD, and taken to the on-line edit suite, where the pictures are conformed to it. In that case, of course, the quality of sound on the system is important.

Any sound card that has separate SP/DIF digital input and output facilities will be good enough for most purposes. That would allow you to take the digital data stream from external digital audio sources, so that your sound never re-enters the analogue domain, where it is most likely to suffer degradation in quality.

Monitoring is important whatever you do. Amplifiers and speakers intended for computer use are unlikely to be good enough. Get professional monitoring equipment (second-hand, if you have a tight budget), or at least go to a source of proper hi-fi audio.

Software

There is now a vast range of video editing software available for the PC – but only five or six real contenders for professional editing. Most capture cards come with some edit software bundled with the card, and it is perfectly possible to do cuts-only editing in native DV for $29.95 if you pay for the 'Pro' version of Apple's *Quicktime* viewer. Editing a whole programme this way is a little bit limiting.

In theory, if you are editing 'on-line' with DV, then you have no need for the timecode of the original camera tapes. Once your pictures are on the disk, it doesn't matter where they came from. In practice, losing track of the original timecode is a very dangerous thing to do, and the difference between a professional piece of software and the rest lies in the way timecode is handled.

Analogue off-line editing obviously depends on producing an accurate EDL, and the editing software therefore needs to be able to handle timecode and to generate an EDL in at least a couple of the common formats used by edit controllers found in on-line edit suites: Sony or CMX, for instance.

Keeping and using original timecode with DV has several advantages. The software can control the DV camcorder or VCR to perform batch capturing: the in and out points of all the required sections of rushes are marked, and the capturing performed automatically, while you go and have a cup of tea or work out how to put the programme together.

The batch capture list, combined with the project file on the system, also provides a backup of the edit. Video editing on computer doesn't actually do anything to the captured footage. The editing software produces a list of references to the edit points in the captured video, so when you save the edit, you're actually saving a list of co-ordinates, and the file is quite small. Those two small files should be able to reproduce most of your edit at any time: the batch capture list will record exactly the same pieces of video onto the computer's disk, and the project file will refer to exactly the same points in the newly captured footage as in the original set.

Finally, if you have original timecode, you have the possibility of treating the DV edit as an off-line edit and conforming the programme on the original camera tapes – Digital Betacam, or whatever higher quality format was used.

It is possible to use what is effectively top-end consumer equipment for broadcast editing; but it is essential, in that case, to be very careful about the way it is done, and to be very aware of what your system is truly capable of. DV editing is possible because the process of copying to disk and back through the Firewire port is effectively lossless. But you should think very carefully about using this level of equipment if the programme involves anything much more complex than cuts, fades and mixes.

In any case, because of the way the DV family handles colour sampling, it is not a good choice of format for DVE (digital video effects) or chroma-key.

There are so many editing programs available now, that it isn't really possible to be definite about which to use. We use Adobe's

Premiere, which can do everything we need, and comes bundled with many video cards. It's a mature program with versions for the PC and the Mac.

Testing

Build a relationship with a 'proper' post-production house. However you work with desktop video, you are unlikely to finish up with a transmission tape. Your output, whether it's DV, or an EDL, will involve finishing in a conventional facility house. Before you commit any serious production work to your system, do a few tests to ensure that you can work successfully with your chosen facility.

You'll find that some of them spend a great deal of time sorting out EDLs that don't work as expected – many of them from high-end non-linear equipment.

One particular thing to note about EDLs is that there's no point in including video effects in them. Anything more complicated than a dissolve or fade should be removed from the edit after you've made the viewing tape, but before the EDL is generated, because there's no standard way of giving DVE instructions through an edit controller. Those effects will have to be set up 'by hand' in the on-line suite.

If you work with one facility house, you can get from them a list of mixer wipe-codes, so that the edit controller can perform wipes that you've entered in the off-line edit.

I have also found that working with the audio tracks mapped to give stereo sound can cause problems in an EDL. The EDLs I was producing were causing problems at one facility house. It was a while before I worked out that it was because the audio tracks were mapped to stereo, but that I was treating them as if they were mono, so that the controller was trying to do two different edits at the same time. The poor thing became confused. Working the off-line with mono audio, and mixing the sound during the on-line edit solved the problem.

Summary

❏ Yes, you can edit broadcastable sound and picture on a desktop PC.
❏ Decide on the software first, then buy hardware to run it.
❏ You need at least a fast PC games machine with 128 Mb RAM and 30 Mb disk space.
❏ A low-end DV capture card will work, but more expensive cards with hardware codecs are better.
❏ Sound cards should be digital with digital input and output.
❏ It's very important to test your system to make sure you can work with the facilities house of your choice, either for on-line editing of your EDLs, or for finishing work on your DV tapes.

SOUND POST-PRODUCTION

Sound has a vast influence on the way we see pictures. The so-called 'silent' movies were never silent, but were accompanied – in the cities and larger towns – by a full orchestra. The impact of even a small television picture can be dramatically increased by wide, stereo sound effects and music. The impression of quality or immediacy or both, of any film or television programme is very dependent on the quality of the sound and the sound mix.

Consider the impact of, for example, the coverage of a rock event. The 'official' programme where the music and atmosphere are properly recorded has quite a different, much more involving feel from the stories that are produced for news programmes, where the camera work may possibly still be quite adequate, but the sound is, even if stereo, usually grabbed from a single microphone in the wrong place.

Good sound can be a fairly straightforward way of raising the perceived value of the programmes you produce. Good sound need not be expensive, but bad sound will be.

Commentary

Although there is a great deal that can be done with a desktop system, commentary recording for a documentary programme or series normally has to be carried out in a dedicated sound studio, because it is likely to sound terrible otherwise.

There are two alternatives in recording commentary: either you record it wild, and fit it to the pictures afterwards, or you record it to picture.

The second option may possibly give you a better performance, since the voice-over artist can see what the words are referring to. It will certainly take a lot longer to do, and therefore cost more. You may decide that the disadvantages outweigh the advantages.

This does not mean, however, that the pictures should be cut to a pre-recorded commentary. Television is a visual medium. There is a tendency – because it's easier – to write a script first, and then fit pictures to it. This is radio with pictures, and leads to boring viewing. Of course there is an interdependency between words and pictures, but the most elegant programmes tell a story led by pictures, which are supplemented by a commentary. The words are often referred to as 'narration'. It seems to me that this betrays a radio-with-pictures attitude, since the narration is ideally in the pictures, with the words providing a commentary.

The script and the cutting order will naturally have a guide commentary to set out for the editor and everyone else what each scene is being expected to achieve – what part of the story it is telling. But the scene should be cut so that it works with the pictures you have. And the pictures should never be stretched to provide wallpaper for too many words.

It's a counsel of perfection, and there will inevitably be compromises – after all, the whole process involves compromise; but doing things properly costs no more money, gives an indefinably much more solid and considered feel to the programme, and makes it look and sound as if it cost many times more than it did. All it takes is a little thought at the right time.

The most efficient method of getting the best of both worlds is to cut the off-line edit with reference to the guide commentary which is written as the cutting order is produced. Then make the pictures work, and re-write the commentary so that it fits the pictures.

Commentary should always add extra information, or provide a guide to the importance of a particular scene or shot. If it's ever possible to say the phrase 'as you can see here' at the beginning of a line of commentary, then drop the line. If the audience can see it, they don't need to be told that they can see it.

Once the commentary has been finalized and the text agreed with everyone who needs to have a say, go into the studio and record it before the final picture edit – before the auto-conform if the process is an off-line/on-line process, or before the programme is played to tape if it's a DV edit.

The pacing of the reading by the voice-over artist will differ slightly from that of the guide. Preparing timings for the most critical paragraphs will ensure that nothing can go badly wrong. The pictures can then be adjusted slightly as necessary, so that the commentary as recorded fits as it should. This method is a good deal kinder on the budget than recording commentary to picture – particularly if you have a large amount to do. Be aware, too, that some voice-over artists are excellent at recording to picture. Others are not.

Summary

❑ The quality of the programme sound can have an enormous effect on the way the programme is perceived.

❑ Always use stereo music and effects.

❑ Write commentary to fit the picture. Recording it wild and making minor picture adjustments if necessary is the most cost-efficient way of working.

RIGHTS AND CLEARANCES

Music rights

I've talked about the importance of music to the impact of the programme. Those remarks apply to every programme, whatever its budget. The question of where the music comes from is of primary importance to producers attempting to make programmes with the greatest cost-efficiency.

In a nutshell, the use of music in any film or television production is a minefield which can turn out to be very costly if mistakes are made. As ever, ignorance is no excuse. If there is any doubt, ask a copyright lawyer.

The most important rule to remember with music and with the use of archive film (by which I mean any footage at all that you use in your programme that was produced by someone else) is the **someone owns the copyright**. Your job is to discover who the owner is, and get their permission to use the material, paying them if necessary.

The following notes are intended for guidance only and should not be taken as authoritative in any particular case. Always consult a specialist if the situation is not clear. Mistakes can be very expensive – particularly for small companies.

Exceptions

There are very few exceptions, and it's very important that you are sure that you are on solid ground if you intend to take advantage of any of them.

Public domain

A work that is out of copyright is in the public domain. That is, anyone may use it for any purpose. Copyright in Europe subsists for 70 years from the death of the author, or the date of publication in the case of a film or television programme (recently raised from 50 years).

The texts of Shakespeare's plays are clearly in the public domain. Those of George Bernard Shaw are not. The copyright in George Gershwin's songs expired under the original copyright law, but are now once again in copyright since the term of copyright was extended.

So far so simple. However, copyright of the author is not the only issue. In the case of a film or television programme, the work itself may be out of copyright (as most of Chaplin's movies are, for example), but you will still have to pay for access to the copy you use in order to make your programme.

NASA has voluntarily placed all its film, video and stills in the public domain. If you call them to ask for permission to use something they are mystified. But that does not mean that it costs nothing to include Space Shuttle footage in your programme. You still have to get the footage from somewhere, and pay any technical costs (copies and transport), and any rights of access the holder of the tape feels that they can demand.

In the case of older feature films the situation can be very complicated, in that libraries of movies have been sold and re-sold so often over the years that it can be very hard to track down the current copyright-holder.

Other general exceptions

- ❏ **'Fair dealing' for the purposes of review** – short extracts of film or music can be used without clearance for the purposes of review or discussion without asking permission – although it's still much safer to ask permission first.

- ❏ **Background music** – if an interview is being filmed at a rock festival, you are not expected to clear the music being played in the background, unless you intend to use the music as an integral part of your programme. However, if it would be in your power to ask for the music to be stopped then you should stop it. Apart from anything else, it will make editing easier for you.

There is a common misconception that 30 seconds of music, or some such small amount, can be used under any circumstances without payment. I've heard this in several forms. Don't believe it.

Music copyright

The use of recorded music is particularly complicated because it involves not one but several copyright holders. The composer, performers, and publishers all hold separate rights, and need to be consulted separately if clearance is to be obtained.

Blanket arrangements

The BBC and other large broadcasters have blanket deals with music royalty collection societies which enable them to use any music they wish, providing details are properly returned, in exchange for an (enormous) overall annual payment which is then divided up among the copyright holders. If your programme is fully commissioned by an organization which has such a deal in place, then you have little to worry about.

However, these blanket deals apply only to the UK. If you are selling your programme in the rest of the world, then music rights still have to be cleared.

This is important. If decisions on clearances are not made by the time the programme is completed, you may find that subsequent sales are not worth making because the cost of additional payments to music and archive film copyright holders, and to actors or writers, are more than the sale is worth.

MCPS

An easy way around all this is to use library music which comes under the umbrella of the Mechanical Copyright Protection Society (MCPS). This includes everything produced by music libraries. A standard fee is charged for standard types of music usage in units of 30 seconds. The same piece of music used in three different places attracts three charges.

MCPS library music is very cost-effective for one-off programmes. The quality of the music available can be variable, but has improved enormously in recent years.

However, the cost can add up quite quickly. If a series has a 45-second title sequence and a minute of end credits, that's four payment units. By the time you've paid for even UK rights on a 13 part series it adds up to quite a lot of money. Particularly since, if the series is to be sold worldwide, it's considerably cheaper to clear and pay for world rights all at once, rather than territory by territory.

Incidentally, in the context of copyright, it's worth bearing in mind that many countries of the Far East are not signatories to the international copyright conventions. If you want to be sure of maximizing revenue from your productions, sell to these countries last.

Commissioning music

World rights on one episode's title music (four units) will cost around £1400. If the series runs to 13 episodes, the bill comes to £18,200. It's much cheaper to commission a composer to write music specially for you, in which you own all the rights.

It's not hard to find a composer. It seems sometimes that every second e-mail I receive is from another composer looking for commissions. But be careful. As in the case of video, the availability of low-cost technology has had a powerfully democratizing effect, making the tools for professional music production available to everyone. That doesn't turn everyone who has a sequencer program on their PC into Beethoven.

However good the sampled instruments on a sequencer are, the musician still has to be able to play them. There are many elements that make up the distinctive sound of an instrument, not just the sound of a single tone. In fact, the sound of the single tone is sometimes the least of it. Experiments have been done which have shown that if you cut off the attack – the beginning of a note – and play just the tone itself, even professional orchestral musicians often can't tell the difference between a trumpet and a violin.

There's no point in using the sound of a trumpet if you play it like a piano. It will sound wrong.

It's always obvious when real instruments are used. One way in which music can increase the perceived value of a programme is in the use of at least some real instruments amongst the sampled sounds. It doesn't matter whether they are electric or acoustic, there's still a different feel to the music.

The most cost-effective way to have new music for your programme is to agree a total price for writing and performing/conducting. Quite likely it doesn't matter to you how the music is produced. You just need a DAT tape or a CD with the right sounds on it to drop into the programme.

Make it clear that you are buying out all rights for the sum agreed. If there's enough of the right kind of music, you can always release it in CD form once your series is successful.

For the right kind of programme it might be mutually beneficial for you to commission music from an up and coming rock band. They get the kind of exposure for their music that they couldn't afford to buy, and the programme acquires a distinctive sound with a direct appeal to its target audience.

Other rights

A number of people other than musicians can often expect payment from the proceeds of further sales of a programme. It's important to be very clear from the beginning in the programme's dealings and contracts with writers, actors, directors, producers, exactly what rights are being paid for in the basic price.

If the programme is being fully paid for by a broadcaster in one country, and there's little likelihood of it ever being sold elsewhere, then it's reasonable that your contracts will only deal with showings in the country of origin. It's still important to be clear about how many showings of the programme are being paid for. In the old days of two big networks, programmes rarely had more than two showings, and residuals were paid on further transmissions. Cable and satellite television works in a totally different way. A programme may have four or more showings in one year. The basic production cost should include any number of showings in the country of origin.

It's up to the producer whether or not to pay in advance for overseas sales. **In any case, the right to sell the programme anywhere in the world on any medium must be cleared.** Whether it's paid for at the time of production or later is a separate decision. It will always be cheaper in the long run to pay for a buyout of all rights, but that may not be practicable on the budget available for production.

Summary

❑ Music is expensive.
❑ Someone else owns rights in everything you didn't produce yourself, and you need to find out who and how much they want to be paid if you want to use their material.
❑ It's often cheaper to commission music than to use library music – particularly since world rights in all media should always be cleared, even if not paid for, at the time of production.

Epilogue

The media world we know now is so different from that of our parents as to be unrecognizable. Forms of communication are taken for granted now which didn't exist even twenty years ago, and the way in which we receive our daily dose of information or entertainment will continue to change in ways we can guess at, but not predict.

One thing that is certain is that the choice of sources for this information and entertainment has multiplied a thousand times during our lifetimes. Whether this multiplicity of sources is matched by an equal multiplicity of content is a different debate. It often seems that there are 200 channels simply offering the same four or five choices of programming that we've always had.

But the fragmentation of programming and the spread of broadband Internet access has already changed the world of programme-making, and will continue to do so.

The big companies will continue to chase big audiences – and there will always be a mass-market, although its mass is smaller than it used to be. Not everyone wants the work of hunting and choosing the programmes to watch.

However, our challenge, and our opportunity, is also to seek out the right niche audiences and markets. If you can make programmes and make money from a dedicated subscription audience of 2000 members, who cares about whether or not the broadcasters of programming to the millions are interested?

Whichever field you decide to operate in, the same inexorable truth will affect you – the demand for more and more programming on lower and lower budgets. It is bound to drive down the overall quality of programming – whatever your definition of quality is. Ideas are spun out for much longer than they are worth in order to fill screen time, and there's never enough money to do them justice. Everyone else might be forced into making lower quality programming. You don't have to join them.

There are as many ways of making programmes as there are programmes to be made. The availability of high quality equipment at low cost has democratized programme-making, and opened up new possibilities for intimacy and immediacy. But it's not a new way of programme-making. Very little is 'new' in that sense. The true beginning of this greater intimacy was the arrival of the 16 mm camera which could be hand held, unlike its bulky, heavy 35 mm forbears. And it's just another convention. It's naive of the programme-maker and audience to believe that what they are seeing on the screen is more 'real' because it has all been produced by a single person with a camcorder.

I truly don't mean to devalue this kind of programme production – but it *is* only another way, another convention. This particular style is no more the only way of the future than any other style. There's room for everyone.

What I've been trying to do is to show that it is possible to make 'traditional' quality programming under the constraints of low budgets and restricted schedules. The value and the difficulty of achieving this is that, if you get it right, nobody notices your achievement.

If you come away from this book with only one message to work the magic, let it be this very simple one: think before you spend. Think before you get the toys out of the box.

There's been a strong emphasis on keeping things under control throughout this book. Film and TV are about creativity, and some might say that this emphasis is bound to stifle creativity. I would say that, if your worries are removed, because the environment in which you are working is basically under control, then creativity is liberated. You know tomorrow's shoot is organized. You know the production is on budget and on schedule, so now you can concentrate on allowing inspiration – and serendipity – to turn something good into something special.

Finally, don't exploit others in order to permit yourself to be exploited.

And have lots of fun, because otherwise there's no point in doing it at all.

Resources

Budget forms

The Farnham Film Company

Preliminary Production Budget

Title: **The Ghosts of Austwick Manor**
Type: 1 x 2hr film

Based on: 6 wk shoot   22 wk edit
(Canadian scenes filmed in Canada.)

Running time (minutes)	104	
Length (16mm)	4160	
Shooting ratio - to one:	10	
Percentage stock footage		
Footage to be shot	41600	Length stock footage: 0
		Rolls: 104

		£	£
Above the line			
Story rights		32,500.00	
Script		33,655.00	
Script duplication etc		1,500.00	
Dev costs		8,000.00	75,655.00
Exec producer(s)		30,000.00	
Producer		25,000.00	
Director		25,000.00	
Principal Cast		49,500.00	129,500.00
Below the line			
Associate Producer	12 x	700	8,400.00
Researcher	4 x	600	2,400.00
Prod Manager	14 x	800	11,200.00
Loc Manager	13 x	700	9,100.00
Prod Sec	20 x	200	4,000.00
1st Asst dir	8 x	700	5,600.00
2nd asst dirs	12 x	500	6,000.00
Runner	22 x	175	3,850.00
Continuity/PA	14 x	600	8,400.00
Lighting Cam	7 x	1200	8,400.00

STORY RIGHTS

	£	$
Options	1250	2000
Rights purchase	31250	50000
Percentage of budget		
Others		
	========	
	32500	
SCRIPT		
First draft	15162	
1st day of principal	10108	
Other buyouts	8385	
	========	
	33655	
DEVELOPMENT COSTS		
Consultancy Fees	1500	
Travel	2000	
Research	2000	
Office Expenses	500	
Legal	2000	
	=	

				8000
Cam Operator	6 x	700	4,200.00	
Clap/Loader	6 x	500	3,000.00	
Camera Grip	6 x	500	3,000.00	
Sound Rec	7 x	800	5,600.00	
Sound Asst	6 x	650	3,900.00	
Editor	17 x	750	12,480.00	
Asst Editor	17 x	450	7,488.00	
Dubbing Ed	x	600	0.00	
Asst Dub Ed	x	450	0.00	
Stills Photog	6 x	750	4,500.00	
Wardrobe Des	10 x	700	7,000.00	
W/robe Mistr	10 x	700	7,000.00	
W/robe assts	6 x	400	2,400.00	
W/robe daily	10 x	80	800.00	
Chief make-up	8 x	850	6,800.00	
Make-up assts	8 x	400	3,200.00	
Make-up daily	8 x	140	1,120.00	
Hairdresser	x	750	0.00	
Casting dir (fee)			5,000.00	
Prod Account (fee)			10,000.00	
Cashier	8 x	200	1,600.00	
Projectionist	x	200	0.00	148,038.00
Art Director	12 x	1200	14,400.00	
Asst Art Dir	12 x	700	8,400.00	
Prop Buyer	9 x	750	6,750.00	
Prop men	12 x	600	7,200.00	36,750.00
Construction			12,000.00	
Construction Manager	x	750	0.00	
Standby paint	6 x	400	2,400.00	
Standby chip	6 x	400	2,400.00	16,800.00
Gaffer	6 x	600	3,600.00	
Electricians	12 x	500	6,000.00	9,600.00
Other Cast			28,800.00	
Extras/day	200 x	60	12,000.00	40,800.00
Music Comp			5,000.00	

SETS:
Allow
(no full sets - flats etc   12000
============
                                   12000

PRINCIPAL CAST
Kids x 3	27000
Mum	7500
Dad	7500
Pringle	7500

Item		Rate	£	£		£
Musicians (buyout)	12 x	150	1,800.00			
Rec Studio (day: rec/mix)	1 x	1200	1,200.00			49500
						=========
Costumes	100 x	30	3,000.00	8,000.00		
Wigs	30 x	50	1,500.00		SUPPORTING CAST	
Misc Stores (allow)			2,500.00		Allow :	
					80 actor days	
					at £360/day	28800
Stills stock (roll)	50 x	15	750.00	7,000.00		
16mm Film Stock (400ft)	104 x	60	6,240.00			
Processing (ft)	41600 x	0.15	6,240.00			
Rush Prints (ft)	41600 x	0.33	13,728.00			
1/4 inch tape (roll)	104 x	3.5	364.00			=========
xfer to 16mm (ft)	41600 x	0.09	3,744.00			28800
Reprints (10% rushes)			1,372.80			
Stock film lab (ft)	0 x	1.3	0.00		EXTRAS - Scenes	
" " " Rights (ft)	0 x	10	0.00		Allow:	Days
Opticals	x	0	0.00		200 artist days	200
Titles			2,000.00			
Optical track	4160 x	0.33	1,372.80			=========
Neg-cutting (reel)	10.4 x	440	4,576.00			200
Slash dupes (ft)	4160 x	0.55	2,288.00			
Answer print (ft)	4160 x	0.84	3,494.40			
Show print (ft)	4160 x	0.42	1,747.20	47,917.20		
Rehearsal rooms (day)	10 x	50	500.00			
FX rec & Rights			500.00			
Dubbing Theatre (hr)	64 x	150	9,600.00			
Cutting rooms (wk)	22 x	200	4,400.00	15,000.00		
Camera (wk)	6 x	800	4,800.00			
Special Lenses (wk)	6 x	500	3,000.00			
Dolly/tracks (wk)	6 x	500	3,000.00			
Crane (wk)	x	300	0.00			
Helicopter/hr	3 x	400	1,200.00			
Lighting (Wk)	6 x	2000	12,000.00			
Generator (wk)	6 x	1000	6,000.00			
Recorders/mics (wk)	6 x	500	3,000.00			
Audio Mixer (wk)	6 x	75	450.00			
Radios/pr/wk	6 x	200	1,200.00			
Electricity (unit)	10000 x	0.1	1,000.00	35,650.00		

Item			Amount	Total
Fares			21,500.00	21,500.00
Mileage	x	0.3	0.00	
Hire cars (weeks)	x	450	0.00	
Unit trucks (truck per wk)	x	750	0.00	
Minibus (wk)	x	600	0.00	
Petrol/diesel (gallons)	x	2	0.00	
Freight	900 x	75	0.00	
Hotels	1500 x	20	67,500.00	
Loc Catering/per diems			30,000.00	
NHI crew			20,313.55	
NHI cast			4,263.60	
Holiday Credits			16,448.22	138,525.36
Office Rental	12 x	200	2,400.00	
Office Equipt			500.00	
Telephone/Telex			1,000.00	3,900.00
Props		allow	10,000.00	
Animals	20 x	70	1,400.00	
Facility fees			30,000.00	41,400.00
Special Effects		allow	1,000.00	
Graphics			0.00	
Rostrum Camera	x	100	0.00	1,000.00
Overtime (2 hrs/day whole crew)			72,895.50	
Costs of Finance				
Legal fees			10,000.00	82,895.50
		sub-total		860,035.06
PACT Levy (if 50% UK input) Max 4500				2,150.00
Company Production Fee (C4 scale)				113,954.65
10% contingency				86,003.51
6% completion guarantee				51,602.10
2% insurance				17,200.70
		GRAND TOTAL		1,130,946.02
US Dollars at	1.6		$	1,809,513.63

FARES
Air:
Allow:

Principals	6000
Production xAtlantic	8000

Rail:

Allow	7500
	========= 21500

HOTELS:

Crew nights	500
Artistes nights	400
	========= 900

FACILITY FEES:
Allow

Manor: 15 @ 1500	22500
Others	7500
	========= 30000

The Farnham Film Company

Preliminary Production Budget

Title: Dancing with the Devil
Type: 1 x 90 min film

Based on: 2   wk shoot   4 wk edit

Above the line		£	£
Story rights			0.00
Script			10,000.00
Script duplication etc			50.00
Dev costs			0.00
			10,050.00
Exec producer(s)			
Producer			3,000.00
Director			7,000.00
Principal Cast			6,200.00
			16,200.00
Below the line			
Associate Producer	3 ×	500	1,500.00
Researcher	×	600	0.00
Prod Manager	×	800	0.00
Loc Manager	×	700	0.00
Prod Sec	×	200	0.00
1st Asst dir	×	700	0.00
2nd asst dirs	×	500	0.00
Runners	6 ×	250	1,500.00
Continuity/PA	5 ×	700	3,500.00
Lighting Cam	2 ×	1200	2,400.00
Cam Operator	×	700	0.00
Clap/Loader	×	500	0.00
Camera Grip	×	500	0.00
Sound Rec	2 ×	1000	2,000.00
Sound Asst	2 ×	750	1,500.00

STORY RIGHTS	£	$
Options		
Rights purchase		
Percentage of budget		
Others		
	===========	
		0
SCRIPT		
First draft		10000
1st day of principal		
Other buyouts		
	=========	
		10000
DEVELOPMENT COSTS		
Consultancy Fees		
Travel		
Research		
Office Expenses		
Legal	=	
		0

Item	Qty	Rate	Amount	Total
Editor	4 x	800	3,200.00	
Asst Editor	x	450	0.00	
Dubbing Ed	x	600	0.00	
Asst Dub Ed	x	450	0.00	
Stills Photog	x	750	0.00	
Wardrobe Des	x	700	0.00	
W/robe Mistr	x	700	0.00	
W/robe assts	x	400	0.00	
W/robe daily	x	80	0.00	
Chief make-up	x	850	0.00	
Make-up assts	x	400	0.00	
Make-up daily	x	140	0.00	
Hairdresser	x	750	0.00	
Casting dir (fee)				
Prod Account (fee)				
Cashier	x	200	0.00	
Projectionist	x	200	0.00	15,600.00
Art Director	x	1200	0.00	
Asst Art Dir	x	700	0.00	
Prop Buyer	x	750	0.00	
Prop men	x	600	0.00	0.00
Construction				
Construction Manager	x	750	0.00	
Standby paint	x	400	0.00	
Standby chip	x	400	0.00	0.00
Gaffer	2 x	750	1,500.00	
Electricians	x	500	0.00	1,500.00
::				
Other Cast			3,875.00	
Extras/day	50 x	60	3,000.00	6,875.00
Music Compose & record			2,500.00	
Musicians (buyout)	x	150	0.00	
Rec Studio (day: rec/mix)	x	1200	0.00	2,500.00

SETS:
Allow
(no full sets - flats etc)

===============
0

PRINCIPAL CAST
5 Characters 2 weeks
at 620/wk

6200

===============
6200

					£	£
Costumes (allow)	1	x	500	500.00	500.00	
Wigs		x	50	0.00		
Misc Stores (allow)						
Stills stock (roll)		x	15	0.00		
Tapes stock	50	x	12	600.00	600.00	
Rehearsal rooms (day)		x	50	0.00		
FX rec & Rights						
Cutting rooms (wk) FFC gear		x		0.00		
On-line finishing	12	x	150	1,800.00	1,800.00	
Camera Kit (wk)	2	x	1200	2,400.00		
Special Lenses (wk)		x	500	0.00		
Dolly/tracks (wk)	2	x	300	600.00		
Crane (wk)		x	300	0.00		
Helicopter/hr		x	400	0.00		
Lighting (Wk)	2	x	200	400.00		
Generator (wk)		x	1000	0.00		
Recorders/mics (wk) - in camera kit		x	500	0.00		
Audio Mixer (wk)		x	75	0.00		
Radios/pr/wk		x	200	0.00		
Electricity (unit)		x	0.1	0.00	3,400.00	
Fares	4	x	250	1,000.00		
Mileage	2000	x	0.3	600.00		
Hire cars (weeks)		x	450	0.00		
Unit trucks (truck per wk)		x	750	0.00		
Minibus (wk)		x	600	0.00		
Petrol/diesel (gallons)		x	2	0.00	1,600.00	
Freight		x		0.00		
Hotels		x	75	0.00		
Loc Catering/per diems	200	x	15	3,000.00		
NHI crew						
NHI cast						
Holiday Credits				3,000.00		

SUPPORTING CAST
Allow :
25 days at 155/day   3875

FARES
Air:
Allow:

============
0

				HOTELS:	
Office Rental	x	200	0.00	Crew nights	
Office Equipt				Artistes nights	========== 0
Telephone/Telex			200.00	200.00	
Props	allow		2,000.00		
Animals	x	70	0.00	FACILITY FEES:	
Facility fees			2,000.00	4,000.00	Allow 2000
Special Effects	allow		1,000.00		Others
Graphics			0.00		========== 2000
Rostrum Camera	x	100	0.00	1,000.00	
Overtime (2 hrs/day whole crew)					
Costs of Finance					
Legal fees				0.00	
	sub-total			68,825.00	
PACT Levy from UK broadcaster input. Max 4500				0.00	
10% contingency				6,882.50	
6% completion guarantee					
2% insurance			=	1,376.50	
	GRAND TOTAL			77,084.00	
US Dollars at	1.6		$	123,334.40	

Title: **Cookery Clinic**

Based on 4 studio days, 2 insert location days, 2 off-line edit days, 4 hrs on-line

	Qty		Rate	£		ACTUAL
Producer/Insert Director (IL)				3,000.00	John	3,000.00
Studio Director (JA)				3,000.00	Ian	3,000.00
Researcher	0	x	120	0.00	Helen	1,000.00
Prod Asst	4	x	600	2,400.00	Heather	1,200.00
				8,400.00		8,200.00
Cameraman	2	x	220	440.00		
Camera Asst		x	120	0.00		
Sound Recordist	2	x	170	340.00		
Spark	0	x	100	0.00		
Overtime		x	208.13	0.00		
Camera Kit	2	x	300	600.00		
Extra lenses	0	x	75	0.00		
Dolly		x	70	0.00		
Extra lights	0	x	30	0.00		
Autocue	0	x	250	0.00		
Facility Fees	0	x	0	0.00		
				1,380.00		1,300.00
Rostrum Camera		x	125	0.00		
Comm Studio		x	50	0.00		
Telecine	0	x	150	0.00		
Tape xfers	8	x	20	160.00		
Off-line edit	2	x	100	200.00		300.00
On-line edit	4	x	100	400.00		1,449.00
Copies		x	50	0.00		668.00
Studio Package	4	x	6000	24,000.00		24,750.00
Tape stock (inc masters)	25	x	15	375.00		401.40
				25,135.00		27,568.40

Item	Rate	Mult	Amount	Subtotal	Total
Comp graphics/Titles	150	4 x	600.00		200.00
Card graphics	50	0 x	0.00		200.00
Roy Ackerman				600.00	
Actors	200	0 x	5,000.00	5,000.00	5,000.00
Hotels	75	0 x	0.00		
Crew & location catering	12	200 x	2,400.00		1,900.00
Mileage	0.35	2000 x	700.00		600.00
Contributors' expenses			800.00	3,900.00	2,500.00
Tables/Chairs/Kitchen			1,000.00		1,430.00
Misc props/food on set			1,000.00		450.00
Title Music comp/record			300.00		350.00
Stills (each)	100	x	0.00		
Lib film rights	300	0 x	0.00		
Office expenses			200.00		100.00
Petty Cash				2,500.00	2,330.00
				250.00	

sub-total	47,165.00	
insurance 2%	397.00	397.00
10% contingency		

Total	47562.00	
Farnham Film Company	2438.00	
	===========	
GRAND TOTAL	**50000.00**	

Total		47,495.40
PROFIT		2,504.60

Per show	8	6250.00
Per Hour	8.00	6250.00

Title: Cafés of Europe

Based on	9 day shoot		hour edit £	£
Producer	x	250	0.00	
Devt costs				
Book & Artwork rights	x	500	0.00	
Script	x	250	0.00	
Pictures	x	250	0.00	
Producer/Director/Script	x	160	7,000.00	
Researcher	1 x	500	500.00	
Prod Asst	3 x	500	1,500.00	9,000.00
Cameraman	6 x	220	1,320.00	
Camera Asst	x	120	0.00	
Sound Recordist	6 x	170	1,020.00	
Spark	0 x	100	0.00	
Overtime	x	80.00	0.00	
Camera Kit	6 x	400	2,400.00	
Extra lenses	0 x	75	0.00	
Dolly	x	70	0.00	
Extra lights	0 x	30	0.00	
Autocue	0 x	250	0.00	
Facility Fees	0 x	0	0.00	
Rostrum Camera	x	125	0.00	
Comm Studio	4 x	50	200.00	
Telecine	0 x	150	0.00	
Tape xfers	2 x	40	80.00	4,740.00

Item	Qty		Rate	Amount	Total
Off-line edit	15	x	120	1,800.00	
On-line edit	24	x	100	2,400.00	
Dub	18	x	35	630.00	
Tape stock (inc masters)	35	x	12	420.00	5,530.00
Comp graphics/FX	4	x	150	600.00	
Card graphics	0	x	50	0.00	600.00
Voice (foreign interviews)	2	x	100	200.00	
Presenter	0	x	1000	0.00	
Actors	0	x	200	0.00	200.00
Hotels	24	x	75	1,800.00	
Air fares	2	x	1462	2,924.00	
Mileage	500	x	0.35	175.00	
Meals	30	x	10	300.00	5,199.00
Special Props	0	x	0	0.00	
Music Composition/Recording				1,000.00	
Stills (each)		x	100	0.00	
Lib film rights	0	x	300	0.00	
Office expenses				250.00	
Petty Cash					1,250.00
					250.00

sub-total	26,769.00
insurance	300.00
10% contingency	
Total	27069.00
% Production fee	0.00
GRAND TOTAL	**27069.00**
Per show 6	4511.50
Per Hour 3.00	9023.00

Revenue projection

Revenue Projection - TV Movie general - US origin								
Territory	**Region $**	**1st cycle $**	**2nd cycle $**	**Year 1**	**Year 2**	**Year 3**	**Year 4**	**Year 5**
CANADA	47,000							
English		25,000	4,167	12,500	12,500			
French		15,000					7,500	7,500
Fr HV		7,000		7,000				
WEST EUROPE	812,300							
United Kingdom		100,000	25,000		50,000	50,000		
Ireland		3,800			1,900	1,900		
German Speaking		300,000	150,000		150,000	150,000		
France/French		100,000	50,000		50,000	50,000		
Spain		90,000	45,000		45,000	45,000		
Portugal		2,500	1,250		1,250	1,250		
Italy		125,000	62,500		62,500	62,500		
Netherlands		20,000	10,000		10,000	10,000		
Belgium		8,000	4,000		4,000	4,000		
Benelux Pay		0		0				
Sweden		15,000	3,750			7,500	7,500	
Norway		9,000	2,250			4,500	4,500	
Denmark		9,000	2,250			4,500	4,500	
Finland		7,000	1,750			3,500	3,500	
Scan Pay		0			0			
Iceland		2,000		1,000	1,000			
Greece		5,000				2,500	2,500	
Turkey		6,000			3,000	3,000		
UK HV		5,000		5,000				
Benelux HV		5,000		5,000				
Scan HV		0		0				
French HV		0		0				
German HV		0		0				
EAST EUROPE	44,050							
Baltic		1,000	500		500	500		
Bulgaria		450	225		225	225		
Czech Republic		3,000	1,500		1,500	1,500		
Hungary		3,000	1,500		1,500	1,500		
Poland		15,000	7,500		7,500	7,500		
Romania		1,800	900			900	900	
Russia		10,000	5,000				5,000	5,000
Slovenia		1,800	900		900	900		
Home-Video		4,000		4,000				
Other		4,000		4,000				
AFRICA	24,500							
South Africa		20,000	10,000	10,000	10,000			5,000
Satellite		1,000			500	500		
SA HV		3,500		3,500				
ISRAEL	5,000	5,000	2,500	2,500	2,500			1,250
Home-Video		0		0				
MIDDLE EAST	19,200							
Abu Dhabi		0		0	0			
Aramco		0		0	0			
Bahrain		1,200		600	600			
Dubai		1,500			750	750		
Egypt		2,000			1,000	1,000		
Jordan		1,200			600	600		
Kuwait		1,800			900	900		
Lebanon		2,500			1,250	1,250		
Oman		1,500		750	750			
Qatar		1,500		750	750			
Saudi Arabia		0			0	0		
Satellite		1,000	500		500	500		
ORBIT/HBO/Showtime		5,000	2,500	2,500	2,500			
Home-Video		0		0				
LATIN AMERICA	56,200							
Mexico		10,000	4,000		5,000	5,000		

Year 6	Year 7	Year 8	Year 9	Year 10	Yr11-25	Total $	Agents fees	Lifetime Regional totals
	4,167				12,500	41,667	6,250	
					7,500	22,500		
					3,500	10,500		
								1,351,950 W.Europe
	25,000				25,000	150,000		
					1,900	5,700		
		75,000	75,000		75,000	525,000		
25,000	25,000			6,250	6,250	162,500		
22,500	22,500				11,250	146,250		
		625	625		2,500	6,250		
31,250	31,250				31,250	218,750		
5,000	5,000				5,000	35,000		
2,000	2,000				2,000	14,000		
						0		
	3,750				3,750	22,500		
	2,250				2,250	13,500		
	2,250				2,250	13,500		
	1,750				1,750	10,500		
						0		
						2,000		
					2,500	7,500		
					3,000	9,000	1,350	
						5,000		
						5,000		
						0		
						0		
						0		
								71,338 E. Europe
	250	250			500	2,000		
	113	113			113	788		
	750	750			750	5,250		
	750	750			750	5,250		
	3,750	3,750			3,750	26,250		
		450	450		450	3,150		
			2,500	2,500	2,500	17,500		
	450	450			450	3,150		
						4,000		
						4,000		
								40,500 Africa
5,000					5,000	35,000		
					1,000	2,000		
						3,500		
1,250						7,500		29,950 M.East/Isr
						0		
						0	0	
						0	0	
						1,200	240	
						1,500	300	
						2,000	400	
						1,200	240	
						1,800	360	
						2,500	500	
						1,500	300	
						1,500	300	
						0	0	
	250	250			250	1,750	350	
1,250	1,250					7,500	1,500	
						0	0	
								83,920 L. America
	2,000	2,000			2,000	16,000		

Territory	Region $	1st cycle $	2nd cycle $	Year 1	Year 2	Year 3	Year 4	Year 5
Argentina/Paraguay		6,000	2,400		3,000	3,000		
Bolivia		0	0		0	0		
Chile		6,000	2,400		3,000	3,000		
Colombia		4,000	1,600		2,000	2,000		
Costa Rica		1,000	400		500	500		
Panama		1,200	480		600	600		
Peru		1,600	640		800	800		
Puerto Rico		4,000			2,000	2,000		
Uruguay		1,400	560		700	700		
Venezuela		5,000	2,000		2,500	2,500		
Brazil		6,000			3,000	3,000		
Tele-Uno etc.		10,000	4,000			5,000	5,000	
Mexico HV		0		0				
Argentina HV		0		0				
CARIBBEAN	0	0		0	0			
FAR EAST/ASIA	123,700							
Japan		60,000	30,000				30,000	30,000
Korea		10,000			5,000	5,000		
Taiwan		2,500				1,250	1,250	
Hong Kong/Macao		4,000				2,000	2,000	
Philippines		2,500				1,250	1,250	
Indonesia		1,500				750	750	
Thailand		1,800				900	900	
Malaysia/Brunei		3,000	1,500			1,500	1,500	
Singapore		2,400				1,200	1,200	
China		0				0	0	
Other Asia		1,000					500	500
STAR		25,000					12,500	12,500
Japan HV		10,000		10,000				
Korea HV		0		0				
China HV		0		0				
AUSTRALASIA	57,000							
Australia		45,000	5,625		22,500	22,500		
New Zealand		12,000	1,200		6,000	6,000		
Home-Video		10,000		10,000				
TV & HV TOTAL:	1,188,950	1,188,950	452,247	79,100	482,475	489,125	92,750	61,750
	Region $	1st run $$	2nd cycle $	Year 1	Year 2	Year 3	Year 4	Year 5
1st cycle total:	1,188,950							
2nd cycle total:	452,247							
10 year total:	1,657,447							
Lifetime total	1,910,699							
Costs:	1,402,765				1st cycle	10 year	Lifetime	
	Advance:	1,200,000		NET:	-213,815	254,682	507,934	
	Agents:	40,765						
	Spanish dub:	5,000						
	French dub:	28,000						
	Tape costs	20,000						
	P&P:	25,000						
	Finance - 7%	84,000						

Year 6	Year 7	Year 8	Year 9	Year 10	Yr11-25	Total $	Agents fees	Lifetime Regional totals	
	1,200	1,200			1,200	9,600			
	0	0			0	0			
	1,200	1,200			1,200	9,600			
	800	800			800	6,400			
	200	200			200	1,600			
	240	240			240	1,920			
	320	320			320	2,560			
						4,000			
	280	280			280	2,240			
	1,000	1,000			1,000	8,000			
						6,000			
	2,000	2,000			2,000	16,000			
						0			
						0			
						0			
								177,725	F.East
			15,000	15,000	15,000	105,000			
					2,500	12,500	2,500		
					625	3,125	625		
						4,000	800		
					625	3,125	625		
					375	1,875	375		
					450	2,250	450		
	1,500				1,500	6,000	1,200		
					1,200	3,600	720		
						0	0		
					250	1,250	250		
						25,000	5,000		
						10,000			
						0	0		
						0	0		
								80,650	Australasia
		5,625			5,625	56,250	11,250		
	1,200				1,200	14,400	2,880		
						10,000	2,000		
93,250	144,419	97,253	93,575	23,750	253,253	1,910,699	40,765	1,910,699	
Year 6	Year 7	Year 8	Year 9	Year 10	Yr11-25	Total $	Agents fees	Lifetime Regional totals	

Net profits

1 The term 'Company's Share of Net Profits' shall be deemed to mean the amount by which the 'gross receipts' (as defined below) of the Film exceeds the aggregate of:

(a) The actual costs and expenses of distribution throughout the world, including (without limiting the foregoing) distributor's fees, trade association fees, the costs of prints, advertising, dubbing, titling, import licences and visa fees and all other costs which the distributor or distributors may be authorized or permitted to deduct and retain under and pursuant to the terms of any distribution agreement by and between such distributor or distributors and the Company; including costs to the distributor of making changes to the Film not included in the cost of production.

(b) All costs and expenses actually incurred and expended in connection with preproduction, preparation, production, completion and delivery of the Film, fully cut, edited and scored (calculated according to generally accepted accounting principles as customarily employed in the motion picture and television industry in the United Kingdom), including (without limiting the generality of the foregoing) any amounts paid to the Owner pursuant to the Agreement as well as pre-production expenses, charges for studio space, studio facilities, laboratory and sound services and facilities, interest charges in connection with the Film's production, legal and accounting charges, and the costs of all materials, services (which may include compensation to the Company and/or its principals for producer services), facilities, duties, insurance and taxes (other than income, franchise, and like taxes) in connection with finance advanced towards the cost of production;

(c) Any and all other sums expended or liability incurred in connection with the production, exhibition, distribution, marketing, and exploitation of the Film or any rights therein, or which may have been incurred and expended in connection with the preservation, insuring, storing, and/or recovery thereof or the recovery of any rents, income or profits thereof, including (without limiting the generality of the foregoing) accounting and legal fees, the costs of litigation (if any) and the aggregate of all sums paid and payable to any guild, union, labour organization, actor, writer, director, producer, composer, musician or trustee of any thereof pursuant to the terms of any collective bargaining agreement or otherwise (including all monies paid and payable with respect to or as a result of any television use or re-use).

(d) Payments to completion guarantors.

(e) Deferments payable to financiers.

2 The term 'gross receipts' shall be deemed to mean:

(a) ONE HUNDRED (100%) PER CENT of all monies actually paid by all exhibitors, broadcasters and other licensees and users of rights in the Film which are received in the United Kingdom by the Company and/or other producer or owner of the Film as the case may be as compensation for the exhibition, sale, lease, licence, rental, distribution and televising of the Film and all issues and re-issues thereof, for theatrical, non-theatrical, television, cassette or other mechanical device and any other purposes throughout the universe; and the net sums recovered by the Company and/or other producer or owner of the Film as the case may be (after deduction of all counsel fees and all other related expenses) by reason of any interference or infringement by third parties of or with the Film or any rights therein; provided, however, that there be deducted from all such receipts all taxes, rebates, allowances, duties and import costs, the costs of making exchange transactions and transmitting the funds to the United Kingdom, and counsel fees in connection with the collection of revenues; and further provided that in the case of any licence for distribution in any medium and in any part of the world on an outright basis for a flat fee, only such flat fee shall be taken into account.

A sample script layout

This is a page of an animation script, but the layout is fairly conventional. Margins are set to 1 inch all round; action and directions are set full out; characters' names are 4 inches from the edge of the paper; and speech is indented 2.5 inches from the edge of the paper.

JAMSCOOT

Extra legs!

JEN/KEVIN

Huh?

JAMSCOOT

We give you extra legs. He doesn't like the way you look, so we make you look different.

Ext Day Intergalactic League Office Block

Tilt down the very tall tower (which is a kind of mix of the Empire State Building, a coral reef, and Walt Disney's idea of a castle in Europe) to find the sign: 'FZI Intergalactic Federation'.

Jamscoot's vehicle lands in front of the building. As soon as they come to a stop, two Windscreen Washer Creatures appear as if from nowhere and begin washing the windows. Jamscoot and Jen get out, and shoo the Windscreen Washers away.

Jamscoot continues from the previous scene, voice-over.

JAMSCOOT (cont)

Once he accepts you with extra legs, he can't change his mind just because you look different.

Jen and Jamscoot lean over the vehicle and help a very strange creature get out — lots of legs, big polka-spots, eyes on stalks. They guide it towards the front door of the building.

Int Day Intergalactic League Reception Area

Kevin's pov (through the eye-holes of the costume) as he unsteadily approaches the security creature.

Mid-shot: Jamscoot, Jen and the Kevcreature announce themselves.

JAMSCOOT

We're to see the President. We're a bit late.

The Security Creature holds up a thin screen and peers at it with all his eyes.

SECURITY CREATURE

Nope.

A sample marked-up transcript page

Edith Winckler

. . . but that was the before. Course, years ago it was different. Them houses weren't here then. We had fields. But he was always a little bit mad.

Interviewer

So tell me again about what you saw that night . . . was it . . .

Edith Winckler   (EW2)

It was scary I can tell you that. (Coughs) Well, I was coming home like usual. Not quite dark it was down the lane, and I just got to the corner of the road down there when I saw it.

Interviewer

Yes?

Edith Winckler

I didn't believe it myself at first. But it was Jed alright. He was . . . kind of . . . glowing. It was a sort of green colour. And he looked really happy. I hadn't seen him like that for a long time. Not since . . . well, never mind. Could you pass me that water now, dear? Thank you (drinks) So I says to him, 'Where've you   (EW3) been, Jed?' and he says he's been places he never imagined. It was amazing, he says, and they're really friendly and don't want to invade the world at all. They just want to help us. That's what he says, anyhow. Course, we all thought he was completely off his head. But he was a much nicer person after than he had been before. Kind of – serene.

Interviewer

Why do you think that was?

Edith Winckler

I don't know.

Interviewer

What did he do then?

Edith Winckler

He moved away after a while. Said he had work to do
and there was places he had to be. You know, dear,
the thing what surprised us all the most was that he

Cutting order

Pre-title sequence – 1950s flying saucer footage
DM7
Commentary
The Search for Extra-Terrestrial Intelligence has succeeded at
last. But some people have known all along . . . etc.
FG8
EM10
HH4
Scary music. Twilight shots of the village.
JK7
OP23
Then, one night, it all changed.
EM2
Shot of Jed here.
EM3
and so on . . .

Media directories

There are many of these. The following two will give you a good start:

The Guardian Media Guide
A directory of everything to do with media in the UK, including contacts for research. Essential.

Fourth Estate, 6 Salem Road, London, W2 4BU
020 7727 8993

The Knowledge
The best of the film and TV industry directories (in my opinion). Includes lots of useful articles on problematic areas such as the legal aspects of working with children.

Miller Freeman Information Services,
Riverbank House, Angel Lane, Tonbridge, TN9 1SE
01732 377591

UK TV stations

An up-to-date list of commissioning editors is maintained on my company's web site: http://www.farnfilm.com

Terrestrial

Anglia Television
Anglia House
Norwich
NR1 3JG
01603 615151

BBC Television
Television Centre
Wood Lane
London
W12 7RJ
020 8743 8000

Carlton Television
101 St Martins Lane
London
WC2N 4AZ
020 7240 4000

Carlton Central
Central Court
Gas St
Birmingham
B1 2JJ
0121 643 9898

Channel 4 Television
124 Horseferry Rd
London
SW1P 2TX
020 7396 4444

Channel 5
22 Long Acre
London
WC2E 9LY
020 7550 5555

Channel Television
The Television Centre
La Pouquelaye
St Helier
Jersey
01534 68999

GMTV
The London Television Centre
Upper Ground
London
SE1 9TT
020 7827 7000

Grampian Television
Queens Cross
Aberdeen
AB15 4XJ
01224 846846

Granada Television
Quay St
Manchester
M60 9EA
0161 832 7211

HTV
The Television Centre
Culverhouse Cross
Cardiff
CF5 6JX
029 20 590590

ITN
200 Gray's Inn Rd
London
WC1 8XZ
020 7833 3000

ITV Network Centre
200 Gray's Inn Rd
London
WC1X 8HF
020 7843 8000

London Weekend Television
The London Television Centre
Upper Ground
London
SE1 9LT
020 7620 1620

Meridian Broadcasting
Television Centre
Northam
Southampton
SO14 0PZ
023 80 222 555

S4C
Parc-Ty-Glas
Llanishen
Cardiff
CF4 5DU
029 20 747 444

Scottish Television
Cowgaddens
Glasgow
G2 3PR
0141 300 3000

Tyne Tees Television
Television Centre
City Rd
Newcastle upon Tyne
NE1 2AL
0191 261 0181

Ulster Television
Havelock House
Ormeau Rd
Belfast
BT7 1EB
028 90328122

Carlton Broadcasting
West Country Region
Western Wood Way
Langage Science Park
Plymouth
PL7 5BQ
01752 333333

Yorkshire-Tyne Tees Television
The Television Centre
Leeds
LS3 1JS
0113 243 8283

Satellite and cable (selected)

British Sky Broadcasting
6 Centaur's Business Park
Grant Way
Isleworth
TW7 5QD
020 7705 3000

Cartoon Network
18 Soho Square
London
W1V 5FD
020 7478 1000

Discovery Networks Europe
160 Great Portland St
London
W1N 5TB
020 7462 3600

Disney Channel
Beaumont House
Kensington Village
London
W14 8TS
020 8222 1000

Flextech Television
(Challenge TV; Trouble; Bravo; living)
160 Great Portland St
London
W1N 5TB
020 7299 5000

MTV
M T V EUROPE
Breakfast TV Centre
Hawley Crescent
London
NW1 8TT
020 7284 7777

Nickelodeon
15–18 Rathbone Place
London
W1P 1DF
020 7462 1000

Sci-Fi Channel Europe
77 Charlotte St
London
W1P 2DD
020 7805 6100

Travel
66 Newman St
London
W1P 3LA
020 7636 5401

Selected UK distributors

CTE
43–45 Portman Place
London
W1H 9FG
020 7468 6688

HiT Entertainment
The Pump House
13–16 Jacobs Well Mews
London
W1R 5PD
020 7224 1717

Itel
48 Leicester Square
London
WC2H 7FB
020 7491 1441

Minotaur International
17–19 Maddox St
London
W1R 0DN
020 7629 6789

Pavilion International
45–49 Mortimer St
London
W1N 71D
020 7636 9421

Internet addresses

No list can be exhaustive, so this is a selection of sites which I've found particularly useful starting places.

Altavista – Web search engine http://www.altavista.com/
British Film Commission http://www.britfilmcom.co.uk
British Film Institute http://www.bfi.org.uk/
Broadcast.com – one of the first webcasters http://www.broadcast.com
BSkyB Production point – producers' access
    http://productionpoint.sky.co.uk
Co-productions – useful French-based site
    http://www.coproductions.com/
Digital Producer Magazine http://www.digitalproducer.com/
Digital Video – American resource site http://www.dv.com/
The Farnham Film Company – my company's site
    http://www.farnfilm.com/
FilmNet UK http://www.filmnetuk.com/
Google – another excellent search engine http://www.google.com/
The Hollywood Reporter (trade paper)
    http://www.hollywoodreporter.com/
The Ifilm Network – Indie Films http://www.ifilm.net/main.taf
Indie resources at Filmmag (USA)
    http://www.filmmag.com/resource.html
Internet Movie Database http://www.imdb.co.uk/
ITN Archive http://www.itnarchive.com/
The Knowledge directory on the Web http://www.dotknowledge.com/
Mandy's Crew Directory (UK & International) http://www.mandy.com
MCPS http://www.mcps.co.uk/
Mediadesk UK (European funding) http://www.mediadesk.co.uk/
Media UK Directory http://www.mediauk.com/directory/
PACT – Producers' Association http://www.pact.co.uk/
Pathe library (UK) http://www.britishpathe.com/
Sightsound.com – webcasting http://www.sightsound.com
The Spotlight actors' directory http://www.spotlightcd.com/
Tanmedia – collection of film archives http://www.tanmedia.co.uk/
TVnewsweb.com – television uplinks worldwide, production facilities,
    newstalk http://www.tvnewsweb.com/

Links to UK broadcasters can be found through several of the above, notably the Media UK directory, and the Farnham Film Company.

Colour video standards by country

Key:

| | NTSC | | SECAM | | PAL | | PAL-N | | PAL-M |

World TV standards

Country	Standard	Country	Standard
Albania	PAL	Madeira	PAL
Argentina	PAL-N	Madagascar	SECAM
Australia	PAL	Malaysia	PAL
Austria	PAL	Malta	PAL
Azores (Portugal)	PAL	Mauritius	SECAM
Bahamas	NTSC	Mexico	NTSC
Bahrain	PAL	Monaco	SECAM/PAL
Barbados	NTSC	Morocco	SECAM
Belgium	PAL	Netherlands	PAL
Bermuda	NTSC	New Zealand	PAL
Brazil	PAL-M	North Korea	SECAM
Bulgaria	SECAM	Norway	PAL
Canada	NTSC	Pakistan	PAL
Canary Is	PAL	Paraguay	PAL
China	PAL	Peru	NTSC
Colombia	NTSC	Philippines	NTSC
Cyprus	PAL	Poland	PAL
Czech Republic	SECAM/PAL	Portugal	PAL
Denmark	PAL	Romania	PAL
Egypt	SECAM	Russia	SECAM
Faroe Islands (DK)	PAL	Saudi Arabia	SECAM
Finland	PAL	Seychelles	PAL
France	SECAM	Singapore	PAL
Gambia	PAL	South Africa	PAL
Germany	PAL	South Korea	NTSC
Germany (prev East)	SECAM/PAL	Spain	PAL
Gibraltar	PAL	Sri Lanka	PAL
Greece	SECAM	Slovakia	SECAM/PAL
Hong Kong	PAL	Sweden	PAL
Hungary	PAL (was SECAM)	Switzerland	PAL
Iceland	PAL	Tahiti	SECAM
India	PAL	Taiwan	NTSC
Indonesia	PAL	Thailand	PAL
Iran	SECAM	Trinidad	NTSC
Ireland	PAL	Tunisia	SECAM
Israel	PAL	Turkey	PAL
Italy	PAL	United Arab Emirates	PAL
Jamaica	SECAM	United Kingdom	PAL
Japan	NTSC	Uruguay	PAL
Jordan	PAL	USA	NTSC
Kenya	PAL	Venezuela	NTSC
Korea	NTSC	Former Yugoslavia	PAL
Luxembourg	PAL	Zimbabwe	PAL

Index